TEACHING YOUR CHILD ABOUT GOD

WES HAYSTEAD

Regal Books
A Division of Gospel Light
Ventura, California, U.S.A.

Published by Regal Books
A Division of Gospel Light
Ventura, California, U.S.A.
Printed in U.S.A.

Library of Congress Cataloging-in-Publication Data
Haystead, Wesley.
    Teaching your child about God / Wes Haystead.
        p. cm.
    Includes bibliographical references.
    ISBN 0-8307-1784-6
    1. Christian education of preschool children. 2. Children—Religious life. I. Title.
BV1475.8.H383 1995
248.8'45—dc20   95-9139
                                                                           CIP

1 2 3 4 5 6 7 8 9 10 11 12 / 02 01 00 99 98 97 96 95

Rights for publishing this book in other languages are contracted by Gospel Literature International (GLINT). GLINT also provides technical help for the adaptation, translation and publishing of Bible study resources and books in scores of languages worldwide. For further information, contact GLINT, P.O. Box 4060, Ontario, CA 91761-1003, U.S.A., or the publisher.

To my three children, who have taught
me more than I have taught them about
God's love and forgiveness:
Karen, Andrew and Jon

Contents

CHAPTER 1

The Child and Christian Concepts

When I was a child, I talked like a child,
I thought like a child, I reasoned like a child.
—1 Corinthians 13:11

"Is this God's house?"

"Yes, Randy, it is."

"Then, where's His bedroom?"

"Where is God?"

"Well, Karen, God is everywhere."

(Thoughtful silence.) "But I can't see Him."

"That's because He is a spirit. He doesn't have a body. He's invisible."

(More silence.) "Is He in this room?"

"Yes, He's always with us wherever we go."

"Is He under my chair?" (Giggle.) "What if I step on Him?" (More giggles.)

"God is rich, isn't He, Teacher?"

"Why do you think so, David?"

"'Cause my mom and dad give Him lots of money in church." (No comment.)

"But Jesus is poor."

"Why is that?"

"'Cause He only gets the pennies I bring to Sunday School."

All parents and teachers have their own favorite collections of humorous things young children say. We try to suppress our merriment at the moment, but then rush off to regale other adults with the "cute thing little Harry said this morning."

Perhaps these childish interpretations are not really funny at all. Is it possible that early misconceptions will stay with a child through the years, distorting understandings and attitudes, creating resistance to more mature knowledge? Will these initial ideas of God go the same route as Santa Claus, the Easter bunny and the tooth fairy? Can a four-year-old, who thinks of God as an old man with a white beard sitting on a cloud, have his or her spiritual development delayed or warped by this nonbiblical image? To answer this question, we need to first consider the basic nature of a young child and how the child thinks. The same processes a child uses in attempting to understand any other part of this fascinating and ever-expanding world are also pressed into service when a child grapples with spiritual concepts.

The Nature of Children

A child often comes to the attention of adults because of some intriguing, seemingly out-of-the-ordinary characteristic. We notice when a child is loud, when a child is active, when a child is cute and when a child is dirty. And we love to put labels on the child that reflect the attribute we noticed: "Hey, Big Fellow!" "What a cutie!" "You're a regular perpetual motion machine!" Each child, however, is a total, unified person—not a collection of miscellaneous qualities and traits. Every part of the child's nature interacts powerfully with every other part. The mental, emotional, physical and spiritual processes are so tightly intermingled as to be literally inseparable.

For example, a child's simple physical movements also have powerful emotional importance. Grabbing an attractive object and shoving it into the mouth is deeply satisfying for an infant. Succeeding at dressing without assistance carries strong feelings of accomplishment for a two- or three-year-old. Running ahead of the rest of the family seems to be a universal pleasure for young children, and a source of great anxiety for parents. Each experience in a child's life touches not just one, but several dimensions of personality.[1]

When adults understand that a child functions as a total entity, efforts to teach anything require an understanding of the complete child. We must also recognize that a child's attitude powerfully affects the learning process. How a child perceives a learning situation greatly affects the success or failure of the efforts expended.

The Developmental Process

Perhaps the most striking aspect of the child's nature is the quickness of change. Blink, and the child has not only changed positions, but also has seemingly grown an inch, learned impressive new words and challenged the adult's perception of what the child is like. Understanding a child's thinking requires awareness of several important aspects of the continuing growth process.

First, the child's capacities for acquiring skills, handling emotions and developing understandings depend upon the satisfaction of basic physical and psychological needs. For instance:

- Adequate nutrition is essential for healthy growth in all areas, not just the physical.
- Mastery of skills and information requires feelings of security.
- Feelings of confidence and self-worth grow out of the many experiences of daily living in which a child succeeds in achieving a goal.

Recognizing these facts helps adults avoid pushing young children too fast. Early childhood is primarily a time for nurturing a healthy body and building strong feelings of security and personal value. Neither can be rushed. And neither can be easily rebuilt once the early years of life are past.[2][3]

The second principle of growth is closely related to the first. Early childhood experiences, both positive and negative, live on to powerfully influence the child, the youth and even the adult. These early years have awesome significance for later maturity.[4]

Third, a child's growth can be observed to occur in recognizable stages.

- Physically, the child passes through stages of lying, sitting, crawling, standing, walking and finally running.

- Socially, play starts out as solitary, then includes another child as a companion in a parallel activity, then grows to involve interaction with one or more children. Finally, play becomes truly cooperative with others.
- Mentally, the child's thought is initially limited to whatever the five senses currently come across. Gradually, the child becomes able to think about what is not currently present, then is able mentally to sequence a series of events, which leads to the ability to grasp cause and effect reasoning. Finally, in adolescence the child becomes capable of abstract reasoning.[5]

There are no clear lines between one stage of development and the next. However, the main characteristics are visible. Adults need to understand what behavior is typical of a child at his or her current stage of development.[6]

Adults also need to understand that each child's growth pattern is not an inclined plane, gently and continuously rising. It is, rather, a series of hills and valleys, ups and downs, yet generally moving forward. Growth in one area, while related to other areas, progresses at its own pace. Thus, at any time, a child may be growing faster in one area than in others. The complexity of the growth process results in every child developing at his or her own unique rate.

Finally, the child's development is profoundly affected by interaction with other people. Relationships with grown-ups and other children are the raw materials of the child's growing view of self and the surrounding world. Other people's reactions to the child, and the way the child perceives those reactions, profoundly influence the child's total growth pattern.

How a Child Thinks

The infant appears on the scene with no awareness of the heritage of human knowledge. As far as that new eight-pound-seven-ounce tax exemption is concerned, Sir Isaac Newton never explained gravity, Thomas Alva Edison never harnessed electricity, and Neil Armstrong never set foot on the moon. The baby doesn't even know there is a moon! All the little darling arrives with is the basic equipment needed to discover these things. And the baby starts working at that task from the moment of departure from that crowded, but comfortable, womb.

Thinking Depends on Experiences

Despite efforts of cartoonists to occasionally depict the newborn as capable of adultlike thought and reaction, an infant's thought patterns are vastly different from those of older children and grown-ups. For example, during the first year of life, the baby can only think about an object when it is in sight. Demonstrate this fact by letting a baby focus on an object, then cover it from view. The infant will act as though the object never existed. As the months pass, the baby may gradually begin to show signs of distress when the object is hidden. However, it is usually not until the first half of the second year that the child will begin searching for the object. A child must have considerable experience with objects appearing and disappearing before he or she becomes able to think about an object when it is not present.[7]

Another interesting illustration of how the baby's self-awareness changes occurs when a mirror is held in front of the infant's face. In the first few months of life, babies show little or no interest in their reflections. Once they start holding items, the shiny mirror becomes something to grab and try to bring to the mouth. Then comes the day when the baby notices the face peering back. For a period of time, there is no indication the baby realizes whose face it is. Try removing the mirror and discreetly placing a smudge of rouge, lipstick or charcoal on the baby's nose, chin or cheek. Then let the baby look into the mirror again. Babies less than a year old are unlikely to notice that anything has changed. But the time will come when the child not only sees the smudge, but wipes at his or her face, indicating a new degree of self-awareness.

Similarly, the infant also seems to be limited in the ability to effectively distinguish his or her existence as separate from the surroundings. A long process of exploring, manipulating, handling and looking is necessary for the young child to conclude "I am different from all this stuff." Toward the end of the second year and throughout the third, the child works hard at developing a psychological identity, separate from parents, siblings and ordinary objects. The well-known negativism of a two-year-old is one of the means by which a child seeks to work out the ability to make decisions. This growing sense of autonomy is not the result of careful reasoning. It develops from many repeated encounters with familiar people and things in the environment.[8] Without the expanding background of firsthand experience, thinking does not mature.

Firsthand experience with objects and people is the raw material out of which thinking grows. Notice the infant's common practice of grabbing an object, then bringing it to the mouth. This behavior is part of the pattern of looking, exploring, manipulating and handling that is necessary for a young child when fixing that object into memory. As the years pass, the child's thought processes depend on the experiences the child has had. One implication of this developmental process is that communicating truth about God is difficult when presented outside of familiar experiences.

Thinking Is Limited by Perspective

The younger the child, the more difficult, if not impossible, it is for the child to recognize another person's point of view. The young child assumes that everyone sees and experiences things in the same way he or she does.[9] This limited perspective involves more than simply a visual viewpoint directed at the world from a position very close to the floor. The limitation is not that the child *won't* accept someone else's point of view, it is that the child simply *can't* recognize that another perspective is possible.

- No one was more startled than one-year-old Micah when little Elizabeth screamed because he pinched her. When he felt no pain as a result of his action, why should she?
- Five-year-old Karen was very startled one afternoon in a restaurant to realize that not everyone there knew who she was.

A child begins life unable to conceive that anything happened or existed before he or she was born. Neither can most three- or four-year-olds imagine anything actually happening in their classrooms prior to their arrival. Even elementary-age children are startled to run into a teacher at the supermarket or mall. Their restricted perspectives keep them from realizing that teachers have a life outside of the classroom.

This outlook on life, which is powerfully limited by the child's desires, causes great difficulty in understanding concepts relating to the Christian faith. Because a child has nothing else with which to work, pieces of everyday surroundings are all the child has available to formulate an idea of what God is like. The child's ideas about God must fit his or her own expectations and experiences. This child-manufactured concept often has no real relationship or resemblance to the God described in the Bible.

Because the child tends to endow inanimate objects with feelings and desires, ideas of God get treated the same way. God becomes the child's greatest dream fulfiller. Four-year-old theologians can be highly dogmatic about what God is like. Until the child has had many and varied firsthand experiences with different viewpoints, there is no alternative than to assume his or her explanation is correct.[10]

Elementary-age children gradually become able to accept that another person might look at things differently, but the child's own viewpoint always dominates. Often, adults view this limitation as a sign of stubbornness or selfishness, when it is simply a characteristic of the only way the child is capable of thinking.

Similarly, the child's limited perspective contributes to a tendency to focus attention on limited or nonessential aspects of a situation.[11] In the same manner as the famous cat who went to London and was impressed only by the mouse under the queen's chair, the child tends to notice only those things that have meaning to him or her, regardless of their actual significance.

For example, take two clear jars of different shapes and put water in one jar. Then pour that water into the other jar. Ask the child if there is more or less water in the second jar than was in the first jar. Most children under six years of age will answer based on the size of the jars, concluding that the quantity of water has changed. The new shape of the liquid obscures the seemingly obvious fact that the amount of water did not change. Similarly, when listening to a Bible story, the same child is likely to miss the seemingly obvious point by linking unrelated aspects of the narrative.

Bobby sat wide eyed listening to his mother tell him the Christmas story. At the conclusion, he wondered if any angels had been singing when he was born. He resolved his own question by deciding angels could not have been there "because there weren't any shepherds around." In Bobby's thinking, the uniqueness of the birth of Jesus depended on the strange occurrences. He totally missed the actual significance because he fastened his attention on parts of the story that were important to him, and used his own limited logic to connect them incorrectly.

Another way the child's limited perspective gets in the way of understanding is the ease with which a child can give correct answers that are in fact meaningless to him or her. Because a child's vocabulary starts at zero and virtually explodes during the childhood years, the child has frequent encounters with new words and ideas that he or she has never heard before. Because a child is usually too busy to stop and ask for a definition of every unfamiliar word, the most common tendency is to substitute a familiar word for the unfamiliar one. Often this lack of word meanings will be obvious to adults. For example:

- Adelle solemnly prayed for all the missionaries in the "corn fields." She had heard her grandmother pray for missionaries in "foreign fields," but that term was totally beyond her understanding. She naturally rephrased her prayer in a way that made sense to her, and regaled everyone else in the family.
- After singing "Jesus Loves Me," two-year-old Jason announced, "I love Jesus! He's in my tummy!" Obviously, Jason had heard adults talking about Jesus being in their hearts. Not having any idea what that meant, other than that it must be good, he came very close to using the right words.

As children grow older, they become increasingly skilled at giving the "right" answer expected by adults. Then the child receives praise and a sense of satisfaction for this performance. Both the child and the adults are unaware that the child was only repeating what others had said at some other time and really did not understand the meaning of the words just spoken. Thus, misunderstanding is often allowed to continue and no one is aware of its presence.

Thinking Is Limited to Physical Activities
Besides the limitations of this restricted perspective, the child's mental development requires physical objects to manipulate. Concrete experi-

ences form the basic structure of early-childhood thinking.

Five-year-old Marie was puzzled for a long time about clouds. She had flown through them in an airplane and observed them in a variety of formations. However, she was bothered by not knowing what they really were and how rain came from them. Her parents soon realized that verbal explanations of evaporation and condensation offered little help. One day, Marie noticed steam rising from a hot cup of coffee. "That looks like a cloud," she announced. At last the door was open to her beginning comprehension of the marvels of clouds, thanks to exposure to a firsthand, physical experience.

Abstract ideas must be recast in physical terms for the child to attach meaning to them. The little girl who talks of her love for Mommy and Daddy knows nothing of an abstract quality labeled "love." All she knows are the hugs and kisses and feelings of well-being she receives from her parents.

Concepts relating to the Christian faith, many of which deal with the least physical ideas people are capable of conceiving, are visualized by young children in physical terms. To the child, God is a man, greater than ordinary men in highly significant ways, but still a man, usually wearing long white robes and a similarly colored beard. He resides in a specific place and has feelings and reactions, as well as a body, in common with men.

Five-year-old Kaitlyn was asked, "If God weren't a man, what else could He be?" After giving the question ample thought, she concluded logically, "He'd have to be a lady or a little children." Because thinking of God as an animal was repugnant to Kaitlyn, she simply concluded God must be another size of human being.

How Thinking Grows
A major factor in a child's thought maturation process is the quality and quantity of his or her firsthand experiences. For example, after Davey encountered his neighbor's dog on several occasions, he proceeded to label any four-legged animal as a "bow-wow." The fact that some of these creatures uttered "meow," "moo" and "baa," gradually brought him to recognize the distinctions. He learned animal categories by a combination of exposure to the animals and their sounds; he also learned by the patient guidance of his parents while looking at picture books. His maturation is a continuing process of adjusting ideas in the

light of new experiences. If no new experiences occur in a certain area of learning, however, the adjustments may be a long time in coming.

A four-year-old boy who watched a deliveryman bring a large bottle of water to his house every week was heard to repeat the twenty-third psalm as, "He leadeth me beside distilled water." His version was the result of his lack of firsthand experience with a pool of quiet, still water suitable for sheep to drink. Because he was unable to grasp the original intent of the statement, he forged his misconceptions from an event that was within his firsthand experience.

Parents and teachers must realize the child's dependence on experience as they plan ways to provide effective Christian learning. For example, the child needs a variety of opportunities to observe and practice Christian values in action. Adults must provide repeated situations in which the child can give and receive love for conversation about God's love to have any meaning. Teaching that relies totally on verbal explanations is doomed to leave the young child's concepts at the mercy of a limited amount of life experience.

Why Teach Christian Concepts to Young Children?

In light of a child's limited mental capabilities, would it not be better to postpone Christian education until thought processes develop more fully? Should parents and teachers even attempt to introduce children to ideas that often baffle adults?

The Bible Commands that Children Be Taught in Faith

Because Christians look to the Bible as the guidebook of their faith, the best place to seek an answer regarding why we should teach Christian concepts to young children is in its pages. God's Word does say some highly significant things to parents concerning their teaching responsibilities.

Exodus 12:24-27. On the eve of Israel's deliverance from Egyptian slavery, Moses instructed the elders in the proper procedures for the Passover observance. His concern went beyond that single occasion, looking ahead to repeated celebrations: "Obey these instructions as a lasting ordinance for you and your descendants" (v. 24). The intent of the annual repetition of the ritual was to portray physically that historic event in such a way as to arouse questions among the children. Their questions were to then provide opportunity to explain the significance of the symbols.

Deuteronomy 6. In this Scripture reference, Moses presents Israel with the essence of God's commandments, clearly stating a formula for teaching them to children. They were to talk about the commandments "when you sit at home and when you walk along the road, when you lie down and when you get up" (v. 7). Instruction pertaining to obedience to God was not seen as a formal presentation to passive listeners, but as a process of continually using the everyday occurrences of the child's life to awaken interest in the things of the Lord.

The parents were also instructed to consistently "do what is right and good in the Lord's sight" (v. 18), indicating the powerful effect of parental example. *Parents are to give children models to observe, rather than rules to obey.*

Proverbs 22:6. "Train a child in the way he should go, and when he is old he will not turn from it." The Hebrew word translated as "train" carries the idea of discipline, a process of teaching that includes consistent example. The "way he should go," or course of life, is one that is proper and positive of itself, and fits the unique capacities of the particular child.

Proverbs 13:24. "He who spares the rod hates his son, but he who loves him is careful to discipline him." Unfortunately, some people interpret the first part of this proverb as an admonition to use physical punishment as the primary means of discipline. A more accurate interpretation of this statement, as well as others on the same subject in Proverbs (see 3:12; 15:1; 19:18; 22:15; 23:13,14; 29:15,17), show that physical punishment or some other unpleasant penalty is sometimes necessary in dealing with a child.

Proverbs, however, clearly calls the parent to act out of deep love and concern for the child's welfare, never as an angry means of retaliation for a disobedient action: "And the rod of his fury will be destroyed" (22:8). To diligently discipline a child is to be consistent and realistic in what behavior is expected, to seek the most effective approach to correction, and not simply to gain satisfaction for the parent's frustrations.

Matthew 18:1-10. "See that you do not look down on one of these little ones" (v. 10). Jesus warned His listeners to recognize children as valuable human beings who have rights of their own. This declaration fits with His remarkable answer to the question "Who is the greatest in the kingdom of heaven?" (v. 1). Jesus replied by having a child stand in the middle of the group and urging His hearers to "become like little children" (v. 3). Clearly, Jesus had great respect for childhood, recognizing qualities of great worth and inherent value that are central to God's purposes.

Jesus' disciples, however, evidently missed this point. At a later meeting, they attempted to stop parents from bringing their children to see Jesus (see 19:13). Mark tells us that Jesus was indignant when He made His famous declaration on children, "Let the little children come to me, and do not hinder them, for the kingdom of God belongs to such as these" (Mark 10:14). For two thousand years, people have used the example and words of Jesus as inspiration for efforts to introduce children to Christ. Note what Jesus did when the children came to Him: "And he took the children in his arms, put his hands on them and blessed them" (v. 16). Nowhere do we read that Jesus had the children sit down and began to lecture them. He loved them, then let them go.

Ephesians 6:4. "Fathers, do not exasperate your children; instead, bring them up in the training and instruction of the Lord." The first part of this verse is a negative command, warning parents to evaluate their child-raising approach based on the child's reaction. If frustration or discouragement result, the method used was inappropriate, no matter how well-intentioned. The second part of this verse is a positive exhortation that combines teaching by action (training) and teaching by word (instruction). The use of both terms indicates the apostles recognized the need for a balance between activity and spoken words. (Also see Col. 3:21.)

Second Timothy 1:5; 3:15. "I have been reminded of your sincere faith, which first lived in your grandmother Lois and in your mother Eunice and, I am persuaded, now lives in you also. And how from infancy you have known the holy Scriptures, which are able to make you wise for salvation through faith in Christ Jesus."

Many people wish Paul had expanded on these brief references to Timothy's childhood learning—the manner in which Timothy became acquainted with the Bible and began to trust Christ as his Savior. Paul, however, merely commends Timothy's mother and grandmother for having provided the source of Timothy's youthful faith, without giving any details on how they went about it. Natural curiosity, and a certain amount of desperation to learn the secrets of Lois and Eunice, might drive us to bemoan this seeming omission.

Any parent or teacher who has dealt with more than one child, however, has learned the painful lesson that what worked well with one child may go down in flames with the next. Had Paul described the ways Lois and Eunice guided young Timothy, all the parents and teachers for the past two thousand years would have tried to impose those same approaches on their children, none of whom were Timothy clones. Thus, as we find so often in Scripture, instead of being given detailed checklists or formulas to follow, we are given principles and guidelines to adapt to each child's unique needs and interests.

Two important principles stand out in these biblical references concerning children. First, the home is the focal point of responsibility for Christian instruction. Second, effective teaching of the faith is done first through actions and example, then by words. Parental example, daily experiences and ceremonial observances are the raw material to introduce a child to concepts concerning the Lord. The picture clearly shows that the adults living in the home are urged to create a climate that prepares a child for verbal explanations. And the whole process begins "from infancy."

Isolating a Child from Religion Is Impractical

"I want my child to make his own decision about his religion. I don't want to prejudice him by what I think" are the sentiments of some well-meaning parents.

It is virtually impossible to totally isolate a child from some exposure to religious ideas. Even in non-Christian homes, a child will encounter playmates who go to Sunday School, see church buildings in the neighborhood, catch religious programs on television and radio, and hear the ubiquitous reliance on religious terms in profanity. These scattered impressions are enough to raise questions and form perceptions in children's minds. If a child's understanding is left to that child's imagination, distorted ideas will most likely be the result.

For the child whose parents possess a deep faith in God, total avoidance of religious knowledge in the early years is less feasible, even if those parents should desire to arrange it. Their own beliefs influence their everyday behavior in significant ways. A child's questions are sure to come. Attempts to evade answering them do more harm than good. This leaves the child to construct a limited, often inaccurate, explanation, as well as lessening the possibilities of future communication between parent and child as other questions are raised.

Ability to Handle Difficult Concepts
Comes Through Experience

Because a child learns through firsthand experiences, the absence of religious instruction during the early years of life tends to retard spiritual and emotional growth. No one seriously advocates insulating a child from all letters and books until the child is old enough to read. Nor is experimentation with writing implements withheld until the child is ready to write legibly. Experimentation and practice are necessary parts of the learning process. Why should learning about Christian concepts be regarded any differently? Why not give the child many firsthand experiences that encourage spiritual growth and broaden understanding of the Christian faith?

Christian Teaching Helps Meet the Needs of Children

Early-childhood education receives a great deal of attention from educators and parents, as well as politicians. Much of this interest results from a fervent hope that positive experiences in the early years of life will lay a solid foundation for later achievement and success. A substantial accumulation of evidence has proven that early learning experiences play a vital role in all areas of a child's development. Successes in early learning have shown positive results in developing healthy expectations for later experiences, while early failures can diminish the child's belief in his or her ability to achieve.[12]

Although positive early experiences are no guarantee of continuing success, they do set a pattern that can greatly enhance future efforts. Parents who openly express affection and provide a variety of learning opportunities in the early years of life tend to continue those patterns as the child grows. Short-term intervention efforts are less likely to have long-term results.

In Christian education, positive feelings about the people, places and ideas associated with learning experiences are important in preparing a child for later instruction. The child who has had pleasant experiences with the people who teach about God will be far more open to learning new concepts than one whose experiences with those people have been unhappy.

Some parents and teachers are so concerned about the child's future that present learning needs are often overlooked. Linda's mother was deeply concerned that her four-year-old grow up with solid biblical knowledge. She surrounded Linda with Bible storybooks and began drilling her in memorizing Bible verses. She knew that Linda's understanding of much of the material was limited, but she felt convinced that learning it early would somehow be helpful later on. Unfortunately, Linda's mother did not realize that a child's retention of things with little meaning or present usefulness is very low. Although Linda enjoyed the attention she got from her mother while learning this material, she began to think that the Bible was all about "long ago and far away"—not in any way practical or related to her own experience.

Can Christian education effectively meet any of the present needs of a child? Linda's mother could more appropriately have met her daughter's four-year-old needs by using a few stories and verses that referred to actions and feelings familiar to Linda. Then, whenever Linda encountered a situation similar to a verse or story, Mom could make effective reference to it. (See chapter 5 for positive suggestions in using the Bible with children.)

Although relating Bible content to the child's life is helpful, adults living the Bible truths are the most significant ways a child's needs are met. When a parent's faith makes that parent feel secure and able to give love, the whole environment of the child is then enriched. The child's essential needs will be more adequately met as Dad and Mom find strength and encouragement in coping with life's frustrations. A child's early environment has great significance in shaping his or her basic personality and attitude toward learning.

Recognizing this fact points out the absolute necessity of parents first giving attention to their own spiritual health. Tensions for the child result when a parent claims one thing but lives another.

A pattern of inconsistency created real problems for Allen. His father read from the Bible about God's love for people, but he rarely showed any affection for Allen, who thus had no adequate model to use as a reference in establishing his idea of God. Allen's father never learned to apply biblical truth to daily living, and passed that failing on to his son.

The child has important personal needs, and knowing Bible truths helps to satisfy these needs.

- Children need to see a sense of order in physical surroundings.
- Children need to feel that life—the familiar world of family, home and friends—is all part of God's loving plan.
- The child who believes in God's unconditional love has a solid foundation for coping with difficult experiences of life.
- The child who is loved at home finds great satisfaction in the assurance that God's love is greater than that of parents and friends.
- The child who feels rejected can find a light in the darkness by discovering the truth of God's love.

The idea of God's love, however, carries meaning only to the degree that a child has received real love from an understanding adult. Confidence in God's dependability is a reflection of one's learning that God can be trusted by having learned to trust those who represent God to the child.

The child who is secure in feelings of being loved can develop healthy, positive feelings of self-esteem. Christian teachings contribute here, too, as the child learns to accept his or her value as a person who has unique capacities and worth to God. By the age of six, the child has developed firm opinions about self. In many little ways, a child shows whether or not he or she feels good about self, either confident to look for and accept challenges, or unable to cope with obstacles that seem insurmountable. This personal attitude will color all the child's experiences and relationships, powerfully molding the kind of person the child becomes.

The child's experiences with Christian concepts play an important part in formulating a basic self-concept. Specific facts or stories have little effect compared to the contribution of experiences and relationships the child associates with those concepts. (See chapter 2, "The Child and Self.")

Investigations into the attitudes of young children and the Christian teaching they receive frequently compare the child's feelings toward parents with feelings toward God. The similarities in these attitudes are striking. The feelings toward God are warmest when the child feels positively toward both parents. Repeatedly, such studies show that parental influence is extremely potent in shaping a child's attitude toward God.

There is no substitute for a good relationship if teaching is to be effective with young children. The relationship between parent and child seems to overpower whatever factual knowledge the child might possess. (See chapter 7, "The Child and God.")

Parents and teachers who want children to grow toward mature understandings of the Christian faith need to start by building warm, open relationships with children. The child's experience of love and respect provide a solid foundation for a child's Christian growth. In contrast, all the lectures and explanations in the world will have little effect if a positive adult-child relationship does not exist.

Notes

1. Dorothy C. Briggs, *Your Child's Self-Esteem: The Key to His Life* (New York: Doubleday, 1970), p. 3.
2. Erik Erikson, *Childhood and Society*, 2nd ed. (New York: W. W. Norton, 1963), p. 247 ff.
3. A. H. Maslow, *Motivation and Personality* (New York: HarperCollins, 1954).
4. Jean Piaget, *Science of Education and the Psychology of the Child* (New York: Orion Press, 1970), p. 127.
5. Ibid., p. 36.
6. Wesley Haystead, *Everything You Want to Know About Teaching Young Children: Birth—6 Years* (Ventura, Calif.: Regal Books, 1989), pp. 51-89.
7. H. Munsinger, *Fundamentals of Child Development* (New York: Holt, Rinehart and Winston, 1971), pp. 268-275.
8. J. D. Navarra, *The Development of Scientific Concepts in a Young Child* (New York: Columbia University, 1955), p. 85.
9. David Elkind, "Development of Religious Ideas in Children," in *Research on Religious Development*, ed. M. P. Stromment (New York: Hawthorn, 1971), p. 52.
10. Jean Piaget, *The Child's Conception of the World* (Lanham, Md.: Littlefield, 1975), p. 376.
11. Ronald Goldman, *Religious Thinking from Childhood to Adolescence* (New York: Seabury Press, 1964), p. 52.
12. Lawrence J. Schweinhart and David P. Welkart, "Research Report—Can Preschool Education Make a Lasting Difference?" *Bulletin of the High/Scope Foundation* (Fall 1977): 1-5.

CHAPTER

2

The Child and Self

*For by the grace given me I say to every one of you:
Do not think of yourself more highly than you
ought, but rather think of yourself with sober
judgment, in accordance with the measure
of faith God has given you.*
—Romans 12:3

"What's your name?"
"Bobby."
"Is that all of your name, or is there more?"
"I think my whole name is Bobby Stop It!"

This active little fellow had evidently driven his harried mother into many utterances of what seemed to him to be his full identification. During the hectic process of rapid growth in the early years of life, children acquire many labels, both verbal and nonverbal.

"He's all boy! What a handful!"
"She's such a pretty little doll."
"He just never sits still. I don't know what I'm going to do with him."
"Oh, what a good boy you are! You ate all your peas!"
"Why are you so naughty? That was a bad, bad thing!"

The list of statements and attitudes people convey to young children in response to their behaviors is endless. From infancy, almost every move the child makes seems to elicit some reaction from parents. These responses have a powerful effect on the child. By accumulating all the bits and pieces of encounters with other people, a child begins the life-long task of building a self-image. The child gradually and continually discovers what kind of person he or she is.[1]

Thus, the child who is consistently called clumsy and uncoordinated, who hears a constant stream of "Be careful...watch out! You'll spill it...no, you're too little. Let Daddy do it...see, I told you you couldn't carry that!" naturally concludes from such overwhelming evidence that he or she is indeed clumsy. The child, therefore, becomes far more likely to drop things because the constant criticism removes the confidence to achieve success.

The repeated encounters children have with people and things create feelings and judgments about self. These feelings loom large in determining how the child will respond to other people.[2] Self-image permeates the thoughts and behavior of the child, coloring all relationships and understandings, including ideas of God.

Jennie was a first-time visitor to Sunday School. The teachers expected her to be shy. As the morning wore on, however, she continued to remain withdrawn from the activities and from the other children. Mr. Harrison attempted to involve her in conversation. After trying several topics, and having no success, he was rather surprised when Jennie firmly declared, "I don't like Sunday School." Thinking this statement was simply the result of being in unfamiliar surroundings, Mr. Harrison assured Jennie that he understood her fearful feelings. But Jennie persisted, "I don't like Sunday School because I don't like God."

"Do you want to tell me why you don't like God?" asked Mr. Harrison.

"Because I'm ugly" was Jennie's reply.

All of her five-year-old life, Jennie had been unfavorably compared with her older sister in appearance, ability and, eventually, disposition. Feeling unlovely and unloved, she directed her resentment at a God who "made me ugly." She, of course, was unable to realize that it was her parents' insensitive lack of appreciation for individual differences that was the source of her unhappiness.

What the Bible Says About Self-Image

Thoughts Lead to Actions
Scripture consistently depicts behavior as resulting from the thought patterns of the individual.

"Oh, that their hearts would be inclined to fear me and keep all my commandments always" (Deut. 5:29).

"And give my son Solomon the wholehearted devotion to keep your commands, requirements and decrees" (1 Chron. 29:19).

I have considered my ways and have turned my steps to your statutes (Ps. 119:59).

Self-Appraisal Must Be Realistic

Scripture also gives frequent exhortations for people to be realistic in their self-appraisals:

Do not think of yourself more highly than you ought, but rather think of yourself with sober judgment, in accordance with the measure of faith God has given you (Rom. 12:3).

Do not let anyone who delights in false humility...disqualify you for the prize (Col. 2:18).

Between the extremes of pride and false modesty is the concept of honest humility. The Lord Jesus made humility the cornerstone of Christian character. In the Old Testament, and resulting Jewish traditions, humility had usually been considered a positive virtue.

If my people, who are called by my name, will humble themselves and pray and seek my face and turn from their wicked ways, then will I hear from heaven and will forgive their sin and will heal their land (2 Chron. 7:14).

But the meek will inherit the land and enjoy great peace (Ps. 37:11).

The fear of the Lord teaches a man wisdom, and humility comes before honor (Prov. 15:33).

The balanced nature of Jesus' teaching on humility is shown in His statement that the greatest commandment concerning human interpersonal relationships is: "Love your neighbor as yourself" (Matt. 22:39). This is not a call for debasement of self, but a recognition that a person who does not like himself or herself can never adequately love anyone else. Each person—whether 4 or 40 years old—is a person of worth in the sight of God. God sent His Son for each one.

The apostle Paul reemphasizes this concept of self-worth in his teachings on marriage: "In this same way, husbands ought to love their wives as their own bodies. He who loves his wife loves himself. After all, no one ever hated his own body, but he feeds and cares for it, just as Christ does the church" (Eph. 5:28,29). The Bible clearly recognizes the importance of a wholesome, realistic self-concept linked to a deep concern for the well-being of other people.

The Power of the Child's Self-Image

Generally, we accept people at face value, or what they seem to be. We often consider the worth of a person on the basis of his or her observed behavior. Because most people develop specific patterns of action in certain situations, a classification seems to simplify many interpersonal relationships. So a system based on outward activity is the easiest to apply.

Most people are unlikely to use the same external standard they apply to others, however. People tend to make allowances for facets of their own lives that other people may overlook. Thus, adults develop skills at putting on masks, presenting those parts of their personalities that seem best suited to the situations.

The young child has not become adept at such a ploy. A child's feelings are close to the surface, clearly expressing the child's attitude by facial expression, bodily posture and actions. Careful observation of a child's behavior shows how the child's entire relationship to life is determined by self-image.

The child who is expected to succeed, who is given encouragement and appropriate guidance, develops the confidence that makes success possible. The child who is surrounded by evidence of inability and successive failures has a great hurdle to overcome in ever developing feelings of achievement.

Because a young child's thought processes are limited to recognizing only his or her viewpoint (everyone else is expected to see and feel just as the child does), it is obvious that the child's attitude about self is a compelling force in determining the child's behavior. If a child feels happy and enjoys the wonders of childhood, it is inconceivable to possibly feel negative about self. But if the child feels unworthy and unlovable, no other option seems accessible.

Add to this limited frame of reference the seeming omniscience and omnipotence of the adults in the child's life. The young child views the adults as truly marvelous beings with amazing powers. The child has no reason in the early years to question anything adults say or do. If adults reflect a feeling that the child is wanted, and is an important part of their lives, how could the child question his or her value? But if adults make a child feel like a nuisance, always in the way, the child will accept the adults' verdicts as being accurate. The child's concept of self is a mirror image of what has been reflected in the behavior and attitudes of other people.

The child who constantly hears that he or she is "bad," "naughty," "a lot of trouble" or "never gonna amount to nothin'" will accept these judgments as being accurate portrayals, and will most likely live up to the picture. And from that vantage point, the child will view the world and its Creator as hostile. Parents and teachers concerned with guiding a child into the Christian faith need to carefully consider the powerful significance of the child's self-image.

What Is a Positive Self-Image?

A person, whether child or adult, forms a self-image from a host of impressions, incidents and encounters. The cumulative effect of the child's diverse life experiences influence several major ingredients of a positive self-concept.

The Security of Belonging
A sense of belonging is basic to acquiring a sense of worth. The feelings of love and safety that parents communicate in the way they hold, care for and play with an infant help to establish a basic sense of trust. The child needs to be assured that his or her place in the family is unconditional. The child who is accepted wholeheartedly need not fear rejection or abandonment if a performance falls short of parental expectations. Acceptance by individuals and groups beyond the family circle strengthen a growing confidence. A child's needs must be met willingly and consistently for the child to feel assured of belonging.

The Satisfaction of Achievement

A child experiences enormous satisfaction from successfully using rapidly expanding capabilities. Most objects in the young child's world are beyond the child's ability to master, so toys are introduced that the child can adequately handle. Observant parents provide a variety of appropriate things to look at, touch, chew, shake and pound. Each new activity usually produces the deep satisfaction of successful mastery. The three-year-old who announces "I'd rather do it myself!" is demonstrating the deep need for accomplishment. Every new achievement fuels increasing self-confidence. The old adage holds true in childhood just as in the business world: Nothing succeeds like success.

The Joy of Feeling Valued

The first two ingredients of positive self-image (belonging and achievement) combine to form a powerful third force. Each time a child succeeds at an activity and receives affirmation from the people who provide that child's sense of belonging, the child is well on the way to feeling worthwhile. The recognition received for each feat meets a deep human need to feel significant to others.

The assurance of being valued is transmitted to the child through human channels. These messages of praise and recognition form a necessary foundation for receiving the ultimate message of good news. The love of parents and teachers, demonstrated in countless small and subtle ways, prepares the child for the overwhelming news of God's love.

Although theologians through the ages have stumbled at the idea of almighty God taking any interest in the menial affairs of people, a young child who has been nurtured by loving adults finds the news of God's love and care easy to accept. *My parents love and value me. So why shouldn't God?* the child assumes.

What can possibly lift the soul of an adult or a child higher than the powerful effect of knowing God is deeply and lovingly concerned about his or her life? This great truth forms the cornerstone of the Christian's self-image.

The Parents' and Teachers' Self-Image

Nourish from Strength

The most important thing adults can do to help build a healthy self-image in a child is to possess positive self-images of their own. Far too many scars are transmitted to children as parents and teachers express their own deep-seated frustrations, ambitions and resentments.

Must parents, then, be free of problems to raise healthy children? Of course not! Parents, however, need to learn how to cope with their own difficulties acceptably. The child should never be used as a means by which adults work out their own problems.

How often has a child become the battle prize in a struggle between husband and wife, each seeking to bolster pride by winning the child's affection and support as an ally in the conflict! How many parents, who feel they were deprived of some opportunity, impose their own goals on their sons or daughters, not recognizing that each person is unique? The child may not have the same interest or need that is driving Mom or Dad. Parental efforts to regain lost opportunities through a child can be damaging to that child's self-esteem. The child begins to question whether he or she has any real personal identity, or just exists as an extension of parental ambitions.

Parental stability is extremely crucial because the parent-child relationship is a highly dynamic one. Parenting is not something adults freely practice on passively receptive children. Parents must continually react to the attitudes and behaviors of each individual child. And each child, even before birth, is a uniquely behaving personality. Within the same family, one baby can be so "good," sleeping through the night, quietly playing in his or her crib. Then the next one may be "fussy" or "colicky" and keep both parents going all the time.

Parents who get one of those demanding, wide-awake-and-ready-to-play-at-2:00 A.M. kind of babies can be heard muttering, "It's a good thing he wasn't our first baby, or he'd have sure been our last one!" It is important for parents to recognize that these physical, temperamental differences are actually reinforced by parental responses.

Parents may frequently cuddle and play with the quiet baby, but they may wrestle and argue with the active one. The placid one senses real pleasure in relationships with people, but the aggressive baby feels surrounded by tension. Both babies will react accordingly. The response of parents, teachers and other adults is likely to continue on the same basis, so the child who most needs calm and gentle interaction often is the one least likely to receive it. Ultimately, this chain of responses leads to some deep-seated attitudinal differences within parents toward each child. Consequently, an unhappy child who stirs up uneasiness and frustration may begin to feel unlovable.

In the same way, parents who have unresolved emotional problems can transmit these fears and frustrations to their children early in life. "The quality of feeding and handling associated with mothering helps the infant to develop a sense of trust in the earliest months of life....It is on this important foundation of trust that a person's orientation toward others and toward his environment is to be built."[3]

Just as a person who was abused as a child is at a higher-than-average risk to also become an abuser, the man or woman who lacks a sense of personal value and worth will tend to transmit those qualities to the growing child's self-image. It will thus be very difficult to help a child develop wholesome feelings about self. A basic principle of child nurturing is: "You nourish from overflow, not from emptiness."[4] For the sake of a strong, long-lasting relationship, parents and teachers must learn to meet their emotional needs by their own efforts, and not depend on children to fill voids.

At this specific point in parenting, many people find their Christian faith especially meaningful. A vital, confident relationship with Jesus Christ gives people a new perspective of their own worth as human beings. To the Christian, no concept is more conducive to a positive feeling about self than the belief that God cares personally for each person. The Christian who has learned to live in that assurance has taken a first step in becoming the kind of person who can nourish from strength.

A rigorous self-examination often helps parents and teachers to pinpoint areas of life that may need attention. "How do I really feel about myself?" "How do I really feel about my children?" "What do I get the most satisfaction from as a parent/teacher?" "To what extent am I willing to allow each child to be unique?" Such questions can get the process in gear. Husbands and wives need to talk about such questions together. Parents and teachers should raise these issues with each other. A qualified third party should be consulted if serious problems or disagreements seem to surface.

A person's attitudes and feelings are not set in concrete, but retain amazing potential for adjustment and adaptation. During the years of early childhood, however, basic attitudes toward life and the all-important feeling about self are established. Only with diligent effort can they be altered later on. Parents and teachers owe it to themselves to exert that effort to build their own self-esteem. But they also owe it to their children to be able to nourish from strength.

Principles for Building Self-Image

The adult who has come to grips with the development of his or her own self-image needs to begin establishing appropriate guidelines to help a child acquire a positive self-concept.

An obviously tired young mother was waiting in line at an airport while her five-year-old twin boys made themselves obnoxious by running and screaming through the concourse. Aware that her boys were attracting a great deal of unfavorable comments from fellow passengers, the mother would occasionally proffer a weak, "Settle down now, boys," which had absolutely no effect on their raucous behavior. The boys were very aware that, at that moment at least, what mother said and what mother intended to enforce were two different things. And the look in the mother's eyes showed she knew well that she faced a long flight with two small tyrants whom she was unable to control.

Parenthood under these conditions is not only unenjoyable, but it is also a wearisome duty that erodes the self-esteem of the parent and robs the child of needed security. The lack of security became evident in watching the twins' noisy misbehavior continue. Rather than enjoying their mastery over Mom, her inability to control them added to their agitation. Instead of enjoying each other as allies in a grand airport adventure, they quickly set to bickering and whining. Far from being pleased with their successful rebellion, they truly seemed lost.

Fortunately, adults can take specific actions to help themselves and their children feel good about themselves.

Establish and Enforce Reasonable Rules
Self-image is always linked to interaction with others, and among the factors that shape this interaction are the rules for positive behavior. Rules and standards that are reasonable and consistently enforced help parents and teachers maintain their own sense of identities and give children stable frameworks for building worthwhile self-images.

Too many restrictions, however, can be just as damaging to the parent-child relationship, and thus to the child's growing self-image, as too few restrictions. Rules should be established for the benefit of both adults and children, and should be appropriate to the child's stage of development.

Wise parents realize that a one-year-old needs to explore and experiment. They meet this need by arranging the child's surroundings to allow for exploration that is safe for the child.

The two-year-old experimenting with language to communicate wishes and feelings is apt to automatically answer no to almost any request. Parents should recognize that this behavior is not incipient rebellion that needs to be nipped in the bud with harsh punishment. It is rather the little tyke's attempt to learn what it means to be an individual.

As the child continues to grow, rules need to change in light of the child's new abilities and understandings. Obviously, this means parents and teachers need to be continually adjusting expectations for the child. Much of this process happens with little or no conscious thought, just as a parent moves from holding both of a toddler's hands to holding just one, to following along behind ready to catch, to standing back with abated breath, to chasing after the "runaway" who is off to explore the world.

Guidance needs to be firm, but always suited to the child's ability to understand and respond. Telling a child that a rule must be obeyed "because I say so," is really an admission that it is not a good rule. Paul instructed parents to avoid exasperating and discouraging children (see Col. 3:21), which are the results of inappropriate and inconsistent rules. Acceptable behavior will only be forthcoming when the rule and the reason for it have been communicated in terms the child can understand.

Give Specific Instructions

Mrs. Lasher was continually distraught at the constant state of upheaval in her three-year-old's room. Her repeated commands to Megan to "clean up and put away your toys" produced results far short of Mother's wishes. Finally, she realized that Megan simply did not understand what was expected of her. The instructions were too general. When Mrs. Lasher took the time to work alongside Megan and give her specific directions, one at a time, the job was completed. Best of all, both Megan and Mother felt much better about the entire situation once Megan clearly understood her mother's expectations. A source of much irritation was removed from the relationship.

Accept Honest Emotions

Adults need to make rules in a climate of honest acceptance. Many times a child may understand the reason for a decision but still not like it. These feelings are a normal emotional reaction to having a desire thwarted, or having something disliked imposed by someone else. A child's emotions are rarely under voluntary control. The child does not come equipped with a button that can switch a negative emotion to a positive one. Unhappiness, fear, anger and frustration do not evaporate just because Mom or Dad gives an order that they should.

Even parents who recognize how moods and emotions affect their own behaviors often treat children as though feelings could be turned on or off at will. Every adult knows that just saying "cheer up" can never chase a mood of depression. No amount of verbal cajoling by well-wishers can make unhappiness disappear. Yet, parents persist in struggling with a child, labeling the child as silly, stubborn, perverse, disobedient, childish and a host of other adjectives in an attempt to persuade the child to disown an emotional state that is very real and very strong.

Who would be so unthinking as to tell a bereaved widow not to feel lonely because she will "get over it" eventually? Such comments would only add to the widow's emotional burden. Truly sympathetic friends look for ways to express their understanding and empathy for her feelings of loss.

Children, however, are often refused similar respect as they try to handle strong emotions, especially if they are considered to be improper (anger, jealousy and so on). Especially at such times, the child's feelings need to be accepted. And the child needs an adult's help in learning to handle these emotions.

Donny was upset and intent on revenge when Ricky accidentally knocked down his pile of blocks. His teacher alertly intercepted Donny, recognizing his desire to commit mayhem. "Donny, I know you must be angry that Ricky knocked down your pile of blocks. I watched how hard you worked to build it up. I know you feel very mad that your work was spoiled."

The teacher understood Donny's anger without condemning him for it. But she also made it clear that she could not allow him to harm Ricky. As Donny's hostility began to diminish, she redirected his attention to another activity. The crisis passed. Had the teacher told Donny to stop being angry, he would have been unable to comply. He would have thought both he and his feelings had been rejected.

There is no substitute for honesty in a healthy parent-child relationship. A child will only feel safely accepted by adults when the child does not feel pressured to put on an act and pretend to be someone different. Especially when being corrected or redirected, the child needs the security of still being loved and accepted.

Provide for Healthy Activity

In addition to establishing suitable rules that are consistently enforced, parents and teachers contribute to a child's self-image by providing a variety of activities appropriate to the child's age level. As one veteran teacher said, "There is no such thing as a bored two-year-old." If something worthwhile and interesting is not provided for them to do, they will *find* something else. Elaborate toys are unnecessary. However, the child should be provided with a variety of safe and interesting objects to manipulate.

One of the key ingredients of a positive self-image is acquiring the ability to achieve. As the young child experiments and works with toys and other materials, certain skills develop. Learning to get dressed and to tie shoes gives a child great satisfaction in accomplishment. "I wanna help" is a common plea, which many parents believe is only uttered either when the family is in a hurry or when the task is difficult. Although it is true that the young child's "help" is usually more of a hindrance than an assist, the patient and understanding parent will be frequently rewarded with the priceless beam of happiness on the face of a proud boy or girl. "Look! I did it myself!"

As children grow older, the need still remains for alert adult supervision and periodic adult intervention. Children's play, no matter how cheerful it begins, will ultimately degenerate without some adult assistance along the way.

Offer Praise for Accomplishment

Closely tied to feelings of success is the reinforcement that comes with parental praise. Positive recognition has a powerful effect on the behavior and attitude of a young child, far stronger than punishment for failure. Positive reinforcement for desirable behavior satisfies the child's need for attention, strengthens the likelihood that the action will be repeated and builds feelings of achievement.

To be effective, praise must be realistic. To proclaim every action as a great accomplishment can only lead to cheapening the recognition. Eric grew tired of having every picture he drew declared to be "a beautiful picture." He finally asked in exasperation, "What do I have to do to draw a bad one?"

Praise should be directed at the child's performance, not at his or her person. Both negative and positive evaluations can be threatening to a child if seen as descriptions of who the child is. Labels put unnecessary and often harmful pressure on the child. Rather than calling a child "a bad boy," it is better to specify that the action was unacceptable. "Leaving your tricycle on the sidewalk is dangerous; someone might fall over it," identifies the undesirable behavior. Criticism can be a subtle problem when it causes the perception that personal worth is dependent on performance.

Kirsten's father had followed a pattern of rewarding her for acceptable behavior by lavishing her with love and telling her what a good girl she was. Real feelings of insecurity began to appear in Kirsten as she came to believe that she was loved only when she excelled. This demand for performance caused her stress and worry. It limited her concept of self-worth. These problems could have been avoided had her father made clear to her that she was always acceptable, regardless of her abilities.

Adults can express reactions by statements such as "I like the way you put away your blocks," "Thank you," "Your picking up the papers was a big help to me." Avoid attaching value judgments to the child by the use of phrases such as "You're such a good boy" or "You're so nice to do that."

Give Focused Attention

Every child needs frequent moments when he or she is the center of an adult's attention. Adults have a disturbing tendency to look past a child, following the action on the TV screen or continuing to read the newspaper while trying to give the impression that they hear every word the child says. The child is never fooled, however, and such adult inattentiveness announces loud and clear, "I don't think what you're saying is very important." Although no adult can give, and no child needs, focused attention all the time, adults must guard against developing a pattern of being with a child physically, but being somewhere else mentally.

Roger's father made it a point to spend some time alone with his son every day. Frequently, however, the father's mind was somewhere else. As this quality of inattentiveness became a pattern, the father-son times became less and less meaningful to both of them. Roger grew up sharing few interests and having little significant communication with his father.

Karen's father planned his day so he could give her his full attention for at least a brief period. He found that many things he considered ordinary took on a new dimension of interest when he began sharing them with his daughter. One evening, watching a caterpillar inch its way up a tree, he asked her, "How many legs does it have?"

"It keeps moving them. I can't count them," Karen answered.

"Does it move them all at the same time?" he asked. As their examination of the insect continued, he found that, far from being a chore, this interaction with Karen was delightful. Shared experiences brought new wonder to each encounter and Dad was usually able to contribute his knowledge and vocabulary. Dad treated her as a person worthy of being the center of his interest at these times. This kind of focused attention helped Karen build a wholesome view of herself and a lasting relationship with her father.

Encourage Positive Interaction

Young children do not automatically assume that the rest of the world is on their side. As they begin to become aware of people other than family members, frequent signs of distrust appear: screaming bloody murder when left with a baby-sitter or deposited into the church nursery, competing with another child for a favored toy, grabbing for the biggest piece of a dessert before anyone else has a chance to move and so on. Sharing, cooperation and generosity are not spontaneous. They must be nourished.

Fortunately, children do have a strong desire to please the significant adults in their lives.

Parental encouragement of acceptable behavior and discouragement of unacceptable actions lays the foundation for the child's own convictions of what is right and what is wrong. This does not mean the young child will then automatically do what he or she perceives as right, especially when a situation is complicated by the presence of other people. A great deal of patient and consistent guidance is necessary to help a child learn to treat others as people of equal worth and value.

Activities for Building a Positive Self-Image

To ensure that children get enough focused attention from the adults in their lives, adults need to plan times and activities in which such attention can be given. Often, busy parents and teachers lament that they do not have the time to do all the things they want to do with children. Interestingly, some of the most valuable adult-child interactions occur in the middle of ongoing, everyday experiences.

Conversation

Helping the young child develop language skills to understand others and to communicate his or her own thoughts is a major factor in helping to build a positive self-image. In homes of low-achievement children, it has been repeatedly observed that verbal communication is at a bare minimum.[5] This lack definitely has a negative effect on the child's self-esteem. For example, a child needs to hear his or her own name often in a positive context. The child's name is more than just a label to wear. It embodies the very essence of the child's total person.

Three-year-old Karen demonstrated this feeling when her father teasingly asked her if her fondness for cookies meant she was a cookie monster. "I'm not a cookie monster!" she declared. "I'm a Karen!" She saw herself as not just a little girl who happened to be referred to as "Karen." "Karen" was what she was. Frequent use of the child's name helps to develop self-identity. Use of the child's name in positive settings helps him or her to feel good about that identity.

"I've always hated my middle name," confessed one man. "I think I feel that way because when I was a child, I only heard it when my grandmother was mad at me."

As children engage in activity, they often tend to produce a steady stream of words describing their behaviors. This is not intended to communicate to anyone, but is evidently important to their developing thought processes. Adults can assist by talking with the child about the details of whatever is transpiring. Ask simple questions to help a child discover interesting features of an object or situation. In other words, the adult's function is somewhat akin to that of a play-by-play announcer for a sporting event, describing what is going on down on the field of play.

"There goes a train. Can you make a noise like a train? Is that train larger or smaller than our car?"

"You're having a good time, aren't you? It must be fun to climb those bars."

"I'm making sandwiches for lunch today. First we get out the bread. Now what do we need? Where do we keep the mayonnaise?"

"Before we eat, I want to thank God for our food. I am so glad we can all be together, I want to thank God for that, too."

"You have such strong arms to lift those big blocks. What part of your body did God make even stronger than your arms?"

Children respond positively to this kind of attention. Words that identify actions and objects help a child become increasingly aware of his or her surroundings. Talk about the details of whatever is transpiring. Also, ask simple questions appropriate to the child's age level (as long as they cannot be answered "yes" or "no") to help the child extend knowledge and/or clarify thoughts: "How do you feel about it? What do you like about it? What would you like to do with it?" Help the child to focus attention on interesting features of an object or situation.

Just as important, perhaps, are the manifold insights that adults receive into how children think when the doors of communication are kept open. Karen's mother was startled to find her five-year-old going through a new Bible storybook and circling the word "God" wherever it appeared on the page. Stifling her first reaction to reprimand the child for defacing a book, she calmly asked, "Why are you doing that?"

Karen's matter-of-fact answer was, "So that I will know where to find God when I want Him."

One particular kind of conversation to avoid is discussion of the child when the child is present. Jimmy's grandmother brought him to Sunday School for the first time and thought it was necessary to tell the teacher, "Jimmy's parents were divorced about six months ago and he hardly ever sees his father. He has become a real problem because of that." The grandmother and the teacher were talking to each other, but anyone looking at Jimmy could not miss seeing the hurt look that came on his face as he heard the conversation.

Unthinking adults often discuss the most intimate details of a child's life in a way they would find ill-mannered if they were speaking about an adult. After having this called to her attention, one mother admitted, "I would be dreadfully humiliated if I heard my husband discussing my problems. Yet I never dreamed of giving my children the same courtesy I expected."

Besides causing embarrassment, discussing a child in that child's presence is treating the child as if he or she were not there. Few actions can be more damaging to any person's self-image.

Music

Singing is another important avenue of communication, especially with young children. The most unmusical adults can open an enjoyable vista of expression to a child by singing frequently. It's not necessary to learn a lot of songs, as long as you know a few simple melodies and are adventurous enough to make up words about the child's everyday experiences, fitting them to the tunes you know. For instance, to the "Farmer in the Dell" tune, you could sing:

> (Tommy) is glad today.
> Yes, (Tommy) is glad today.
> He's glad because he has new shoes,
> Yes, (Tommy) is glad today.

Vary the third line to fit the occasion. Or, sing, "He's glad because the Lord loves him."

No matter how poorly you think you sing, the young child sings even worse! Singing little ditties to an infant is a great way to set a pattern and build confidence so that singing will continue as the child grows.

Growing

As the child grows, the changes in size, strength and coordination are exciting to note for both the child and the surrounding adults. Share this enthusiasm by using a growth chart, supplemented with photographs taken at various stages of growth. A photo album that shows how the child and others are changing also is an opportunity to illustrate how the child is "growing taller and stronger, just as God planned."

Select a plant or a tree and have the child observe its growth and seasonal changes. Relate the transformations to the child's development. "See how pretty and green our tree is. Do you remember when it was bare and looked so cold and lonely? God planned for many kinds of trees to get new leaves every year. And God planned for you to keep growing taller and stronger, too."

Cut a piece of string the same length as the child's height. Let the child compare the string's length to other objects around the house or classroom. Talk about skills the child is gaining. Express your sense of pride in the many things the child has learned to do.

Physical Skills

Every child is continually facing the challenges and frustrations of acquiring new skills. At each stage, talk with the child about these skills. Agree with the child that learning to do something new is sometimes hard. Talk about the many things already mastered and your confidence that new challenges will also be met.

Toddlers and two-year-olds are not quite ready to put on catcher's mitts and start tossing a few with Dad. But they can do many things with balls that are fun and helpful to physical coordination and that give feelings of satisfaction in bodily control. Also, the activities help the child and the adult to enjoy interacting with each other—a critical ingredient to the self-image of both.

A young child enjoys a great sense of accomplishment in imitating an adult model by following simple directions in handling a ball. Give one simple instruction at a time. "Hold the ball in both hands. That's right! Now stretch both hands straight out in front. Now put the ball in just one hand. Now put it in the other hand! Now bounce the ball!"

An older child will be able to hold the ball out to the side, over the head and behind the back. All ages enjoy rolling or bouncing a ball on the floor. Suggest that the child try rolling the ball up and down and over his or her body. This activity provides a good opportunity to build awareness of body parts, as well as to improve coordination in keeping the ball under control over uneven surfaces. Holding a ball between the feet or knees and hopping (or walking) is great fun and is a good test of agility. Encourage children to think of other creative things to do with the ball.

Many materials have become staples of early childhood programs because of their effectiveness in helping the child to improve physical competency. Puzzles are a challenge to eye-hand coordination and small-muscle development. Blocks of varying sizes and shapes help the child to develop manipulative skills, as well as to exercise the ability to plan and carry out an idea. Modeling clay and play dough offer opportunities for creation with no fear of failure because mistakes can always be squeezed out and a fresh start made. Finger-painting, gadget printing, collages, easel painting and cut-and-paste projects are creative art experiences that allow a child the freedom to create something unique. Asking a child to "Tell me about your picture" often opens fascinating horizons for understanding and growth for both the child and the adult.

In whatever activity children are engaged, they need affirmation of what they are doing right far more than they need criticism of their flaws. Just watch a child's confidence deflate when an adult says, "No wonder you're having trouble. You're doing it all wrong." Instead, praise the child's effort and suggest or demonstrate one or two tips that will help.

Independence Training
Closely related to developing physical competence is cultivating independence. During the early years of life, the child makes dramatic strides from being totally dependent to becoming amazingly competent in caring for many basic needs. Each step in developing independence has the potential for adding substantially to the child's positive self-concept.

Unfortunately, adults often needlessly delay the child's assumption of many functions that would build the child's self-esteem. Sometimes adults actively encourage dependency as a way of satisfying the adult's need to be needed, or simply because it takes too much time to teach the child what to do. Doing things for the child that the child could be learning to do not only delays the child's development, but also damages the child's self-esteem.

Parents and teachers should consciously examine everything they do for a child and ask, "How much of this activity could the child do?" Giving praise for each accomplishment will help the child enjoy the experience and increase the desire to do it again. It will also ensure against the child feeling that self-reliance results in less attention—a truly discouraging prospect for all children.

Games
While riding in the car, ask a child to help you look for a green truck, a yellow house or an alphabet letter on a sign. Ask the child, "What can your hands do that your nose cannot?" or "What can you do with your

ears that you cannot do with your elbows?" Such games can be played verbally or pantomimed.

Parents have been playing games with babies from the beginning of time. Many simple, traditional games are valuable in helping the child develop abilities to perceive and move. "This little pig went to market" is a longtime favorite because it is fun. It is an example of many games that produce growing awareness of parts of the body, helping the child to feel positive about self.

"Peekaboo" is a favorite of little ones. The game can be varied infinitely by using a variety of objects and hiding places. "Hide-and-seek" for twos and threes is only slightly removed from infant peekaboo. The fun of the game for the child is finding, not hiding or seeking. Young children will "hide" in obvious places, call out to tell you where they are, and then laugh uproariously when they are found. They see nothing incongruous about reusing the same hiding place repeatedly, and are likely to become upset if they are unable to find their partners quickly.

Many fours and fives continue the same pattern and only gradually begin to see it as a game where the object is to remain hidden rather than to be discovered.

Participation is the main objective for a young child in a game. Winning is a fuzzy concept. Games for young children should be those in which "Everybody won!" Fours and fives begin to understand that in competition a winner produces a loser. Competitive games are not appropriate for building self-image in early childhood. Even with older children, stress cooperation and participation. Keep the focus on having fun together, not on winning or losing, for in many ways, children's games are the most common ways they learn to enjoy or fear other people.

In all activities, the adult should seek to give the child enjoyable, successful experiences that develop feelings of value. The early experiences of life are highly crucial to a child's lifelong concept of self, and as a result, have a lasting influence on all of life's relationships and activities.

"'Tis education forms the common mind: Just as the twig is bent, the tree's inclined" has long been part of Western folklore. Scientific data supports this view. The origins of self lie in the early years. How the child will see self is influenced by the way he or she is treated, how he or she is evaluated and how the child perceives these evaluations.[6]

Notes

1. H. Munsinger, *Fundamentals of Child Development* (New York: Holt, Rinehart and Winston, 1971), p. 403.
2. Dorothy C. Briggs, *Your Child's Self-Esteem: The Key to His Life* (New York: Doubleday, 1970), p. 3.
3. Bruce Grossman, "Enhancing the Self," *Exceptional Children* 38 (1971): 249-254.
4. Briggs, *Your Child's Self-Esteem*, p. 55.
5. Munsinger, *Fundamentals of Child Development*, p. 384.
6. Ira Gordon, "The Beginnings of Self," in *As the Twig Is Bent*, eds. Robert Anderson and Harold Shane (Boston: Houghton Mifflin, 1971), p. 142.

C H A P T E R

3

The Child, Things and Others

"Love one another."
—John 13:34

"Tommy, this is Pablo, and he would like to play with you.
Would you share one of your trucks with him?"
(Two-year-old Tommy remains silent, and pulls both trucks
closer to himself.)
"If you both had a truck, you could have fun playing
together."
(More silence. Tighter grip on the trucks.)
"Which truck would you like Pablo to play with, the red
one or the blue one?"
(Tommy clutches both trucks to his chest.)
"Here, Pablo, you can play with these blocks until Tommy is
through playing with the trucks."

Sharing and cooperation do not come automatically to a young child,
largely because they are outside the understanding of the child.
Although adults cajole and entice, the child tends to be suspicious of
requests to part with a toy, even for a moment.

Sensing that this possessive attitude signals the beginning of a life-
time of selfishness, concerned adults often become overzealous in their
efforts to teach the child to take turns and share. The resulting howls of
displeasure can be heard repeatedly from little mouths whose owners
vigorously resist these socialization efforts. Much of the strain and

unhappiness of this process could be diminished if parents and teachers realized how the child views these encounters.

The same characteristics of the child that influence his or her developing self-image are at work in forming the child's view of, and behavior toward, other people. For example, the infant begins life unable to distinguish between self and surroundings. Neither does the baby initially recognize the vast differences between other people and all other categories of "other." The people in the child's life start out as just parts of all the complex and fascinating surroundings. A gigantic learning task lies just ahead, but the child quickly begins to make progress.

Within a matter of weeks, babies show a marked preference to look at more complex patterns than simpler, less interesting ones. They also prefer to look at a normal picture of a human face instead of one in which the facial features (nose, eyes, mouth and so on) have been moved out of position.[1] By carefully observing the responses of infants, researchers have concluded that an infant can distinguish his or her mother from other female adults within just a few weeks of birth.[2]

During the early months, the baby refines his or her perceptions, but generally remains unable to recognize that objects or people exist when out of sight. When an object moves, the baby's eyes will follow. The infant will reach out clumsily for it, but if it passes from the line of vision, the baby will usually act as though it has ceased to exist. After about 6 months of age, the child will begin to look for the object that disappeared, but will only repeat whatever action he or she was performing at the moment of disappearance. By 10 months, the child may begin to actively search for the object, but will look only in places where it has been found before.

Jean Piaget, the pioneering Swiss psychologist, asserted that not until the latter part of the second year of life is a child able to think about an object that is not physically present. Piaget concluded that it takes nearly two years of exposure and interaction with things and people before the child is capable of realizing they exist permanently and are separate from the child's own actions.[3]

Subsequent research has supported or refined much of Piaget's work, discovering that infants are in no sense unthinking beings, passively observing the activity around them. Instead, at surprisingly young ages, infants are hard at work, making sense out of their surroundings. Long before they are able to use language, they show abilities to distinguish among objects and people, to remember earlier experiences and to think about items that have been moved out of sight.[4]

As the child grows, these remarkable early abilities are continually called into play as new experiences are encountered. For at least the first six or seven years of life, the child will astonish family, friends and neighbors with evidences of new learning. At the same time, the child has a significant difficulty in seeing the world objectively, which stems from the inability to recognize the essential factors in complex situations.

As noted in chapter 1, the child's attention is drawn to one aspect only, making the child unable to deal with two dimensions of a problem simultaneously. This limitation on childlike thought manifests itself repeatedly in the child's experience, often until age six or seven. Most of the young child's illogical actions have their roots in this restricted viewpoint. The child simply has not encountered enough of the world to be able to think about one or more specific facts and come to a general conclusion. Nor can the child take a general principle and apply it to specific actions. Rather, the child is limited to using a particular fact to lead to another particular fact.

Because the child selects those aspects of a situation that seem most interesting at the moment, the child often relates things to others in a unique, creative and sometimes inappropriate manner.[5] Such was the case when the three-year-old boy boldly announced, "I haven't had my bath, so it isn't bedtime." These two common events had always occurred together in his experience. So he reasoned that one depended on the other. He was unable to see the "big picture"—that bedtime and bathtime were separate events that were usually scheduled at nighttime.

The Child and Things

We have seen that the young child's view of the world centers on self. All the action of the things in the infant's environment seem to revolve around the child and his or her desires. Only very gradually does the child come to see that these things have existences of their own and are not dependent on him or her for their actions. The child also perceives that events seem to depend on adults who appear all-powerful. Things are pushed and pulled, opened and closed, all for the child's benefit and all by masterful adults.[6]

A child assigns thoughts and feelings to many familiar objects. Dolls and teddy bears talk and make decisions. Quite often the child attributes his or her own emotions or desires to these inanimate objects. This aspect of a child's thought process is shown very dramatically following natural disasters such as earthquakes or storms. Young children who are awakened in the night by severe shaking or loud noises often refuse to get back into their beds when the upheaval is over. They are often convinced that all of the upset has been caused by the bed in which they were asleep at the moment the disaster hit. Their fears are directed squarely at the offending beds, having no awareness of the larger natural forces at work.

Piaget noted in his observations of young children that this kind of outlook gradually diminishes and has largely disappeared by age six or seven. Those objects that remain stationary lose their reputation for being alive sooner than things that move or grow, such as cars or plants.[7] This practice of attributing life and personality to inanimate objects should not seem too unusual to adults who give names to their cars and computers, and even talk to them, especially when they malfunction!

Gradually, the child ceases to view objects as being alive in the same sense people are alive. As this shift occurs, the child begins to attribute their movements and their very existence to human operations. This viewpoint is the natural outgrowth of seeing adults manipulate the world in so many wonderful ways. Again applying the practice of relating one specific to another, the young child often sees such phenomena as the sun and moon acting in response to human direction.

God Made All Things

Parents and teachers who desire for a child to know that God "made the world and everything in it" (Acts 17:24) need to consider carefully the way they present this fact. The problem is not one of disbelief, for the young child is willing to accept explanations given by adults. The difficulty is in terms of what the explanation will mean to the child.

A two-year-old will accept the statement that God made apples with the same level of understanding if told that General Motors makes Buicks or that Mommy makes cakes. In the mind of a child, these products are all equally wonderful creations. And the sources are not nearly as interesting as the products themselves.

By the age of four or five, however, questions of origin have become of real interest, and often entail the "how" as well as the "who" or "what." Questions about the process of Creation can come fast and furiously. Some children will be satisfied with "God made it." This answer, however, may carry magical visions of a super sorcerer. Other children will demand to know how He made it, or may deny that He did, because their own experiences tell them the object in question came from a store.

Teachers and parents usually find it best to say that "God planned for apples to grow," rather than leaving a young mind to wrestle with how God went about forming each individual apple. (And once the child begins asking where babies come from, talking about God's plan for families is far preferable to bringing in the stork, or even asserting that "God makes babies.") Any verbal explanation of natural wonders, however, usually gives a child only a superficial understanding at best. Words are the least effective way for a child to learn.

The most effective way for a child to learn is through firsthand experience. The child needs many encounters with growing things to begin to understand his or her origins. Through the fun of planting seeds, watering the soil and watching the new growth, the child starts to grasp the wonders of life. After repeated firsthand experiences with plant and animal life cycles, a child begins to comprehend God as Creator, the One who set it all in motion and cares deeply about all that He made.

Such awareness comes as adults interpret the child's observations and activities in terms of Bible truth. "Do you see any new leaves on our plant today? You found a big one! Let's count the points on it. Only God can make plants grow. The Bible says 'God is good' (Ps. 73:1). I'm glad God planned such beautiful plants for us to enjoy." The sense of awe that comes from these experiences with living things builds preliminary foundations for a realistic concept of God.

Activities for Learning About Things

What the child learns about the surrounding world happens spontaneously through interaction with the materials in the environment. Thus, the adults in a child's life play a major role by the decisions they make concerning just what these things will be. From infancy on, the child should be provided with a variety of toys that are safe, interesting and easy to manipulate.

Toys

Early enjoyment of touching, squeezing and chewing encourages curiosity and self-confidence, essential ingredients for later explorations. The best toys are those the child can manipulate, rather than just observe. Obviously, not having read the instruction manual, the child is likely to try a whole host of creative ways to use any toy; thus, safety is always a vital concern.

Puzzles offer many interesting ways to learn about shapes, color and relationships of objects. Puzzles include the traditional jigsaw puzzle or a variety of three-dimensional objects for the child to fit together or take apart—especially take apart! Although very young children need simple puzzles of three or four large pieces, four- and five-year-olds are often capable of completing puzzles that contain more than 25 pieces. The sense of satisfaction the child receives from problem solving is one benefit of puzzles. Working puzzles, however, also sharpens a child's perception of pictures, colors and objects.

A variety of sensory experiences helps children to appreciate the diversity of their world and to build confidence in exploring it. Recognition games in which the child is limited to the use of one sense are great fun. For example, trying to guess an object just by its sound promotes awareness of the environment. "I'm glad God planned your ears so you can hear that bell ringing." Help a child associate pleasant experiences with God's goodness. Similar games can be played using only touch or smell as the means of identification.

Art Activities

The use of touch is an important part of art experiences, which are usually considered mainly a visual medium.

- Working with clay or play dough provides an interesting sensory experience.
- Finger painting is one of the most exciting and enjoyable experiences a child can have! As a child is enjoying the experience, say "Thank You, God, for Dina's fingers that can make such interesting pictures!"

- Collages (gluing or pasting random materials of differing textures, colors and shapes) have great sensory appeal for children. Fabrics, wood, leaves, cereals, seashells, nut shells and flower petals are just a few of the items that children enjoy touching and arranging, then gluing onto a surface.
- Many of the objects used for collages can be used for rubbings. Place objects on a flat surface and cover them with paper. (You may want to tape down the edges of the paper to keep it from shifting as the child works.) The child then rubs a crayon over the paper until the pattern of the objects underneath shows through.

The child will grow to appreciate God's world as you comment, "I like the different kinds of things God made for us. Some things are soft, like this feather. Some things are hard, like these seeds. God made all these things for us to enjoy. God loves us."

Living Things

Experiences with living things are also significant to the child's learning about things, and ultimately about people. Insects, fish, birds or other pets provide daily lessons in natural processes, as well as help the child learn respect for living things. Plant growth is often of special interest to a young child because changes usually occur more rapidly in plants than in animals.

- A bean placed on a wet sponge lets a child observe the growth of both leaves and roots.
- A sweet potato partly submerged in water offers the same lessons on a larger scale.
- Seeds planted in the garden or in an indoor planter often show fascinating changes within just a few weeks.
- Provide a good quality magnifying glass to make observation a vastly enriching experience.

Simple explanations of what the child observes add to the child's appreciation and understanding, especially when the information comes in answer to the child's questions. "God planned for that little seed to be able to use water so that it can grow and become a big plant. God is so great!"

While sharing the sweet taste of a ripe apple with two-year-olds, Mr. Fitzgerald paused, and said quietly, "Thank You, God, for making good apples for us to eat." The children understood little or nothing of the source of the apples. But they sensed their teacher's reverent attitude of thankfulness to God, a meaningful foundation for future learning.

The Child and People

The newborn infant does not immediately distinguish between things and people. (At times, older children also seem to treat people more like things than as living beings who have similar feelings and desires.) Gradually, as the baby becomes aware that people are unique, people become the most interesting part of the child's world. The way adults treat the child forms the basis for feelings about self and, thus, about everything else, including God.

Christians have long been grateful to Jesus for His practice of addressing God as "Father," for this title has given finite minds, including those whose personal experiences with "father" have been unpleasant, a means of attempting to grasp some human-scale characteristics of the infinite.

We will see in chapter 7 that the young child's growing concept of God is powerfully influenced by a relationship with parents. Studies have consistently shown that a child's feelings toward his or her parents have a strong and lasting influence on feelings about God.[8]

Influences on Behavior
The child's behavior is also significantly influenced by the actions of parents. Parents serve as the primary models for all the child's behavior from infancy on. Often a child will express a desire to "be like" Daddy or Mommy. Most of a child's imitation of parents, however, occurs unconsciously.

Adult encouragement during a child's performance of a task, and praise when it is completed, exerts a powerful influence on the child's behavior. Children are strongly motivated to please the significant adults in their lives! This desire to please serves as the basis for developing a conscience in the young child. Once the child is able to think of his or her parents, although they may not be physically present, it becomes possible for the child to consciously base behavior on what the child believes will please them. Parental encouragement for acceptable behavior thus lays the foundation for the child's own convictions of what is right.[9]

Moral Judgments

Observers of young children are often confused by the seeming lack of a relationship between what a child says is right or wrong and the way the child actually behaves.[10]

Much of what the child can express seems to be merely words that have no immediate relationship to behavior. The reason appears to be that the child is unable to give an adequate explanation for actions until he or she has acquired substantial experience in situations calling for moral judgments. The moral judgments of the young child are dominated by the child's limited view of the world.[11]

The examples set by parents and teachers provide a powerful model for the young child, but the child will always react according to the way things appear from his or her limited viewpoint.

A child faced with rules created by all-knowing adults does not usually think to question them. Five-year-old Karen announced after her first week at kindergarten that "Robert was bad. He didn't take turns on the swing today." When asked why Robert's actions were wrong, Karen's answer was very firm: "Because Mrs. Meyers said we had to take turns on the swings!" To Karen, the rule existed simply because her teacher said so. No thought was given to the underlying sense of cooperation as the reason behind the rule. Nor was the idea of taking turns apparent as a good thing for everything else at school. The rule was sacred and no questions needed to be asked.

Both Jean Piaget and Lawrence Kohlberg identified six major aspects of the young child's moral judgments, which distinguish the young child's thinking from that of more mature children and adults. Both investigators saw these factors as developing independently so that a child may be advanced in one category and immature in another. They found most of these factors present in almost all children until seven or eight years of age. They recognized, however, that both intelligence and specific experiences could alter the rate of growth in either direction.

First, the young child judges an act as right or wrong on the physical consequences, not on the motives of the person involved. Spilling milk is no less an offense to the child if unintentional than if done on purpose. Accidental damage is just as culpable as intentional mayhem. The child, however, does temper the judgments of his or her own misdeeds sooner than for someone else.

Second, a young child judges actions as either right or wrong and having no middle ground. And, the self-centered nature of the child's thinking causes him or her to expect everyone else to share this evaluation.

Third, the child's judgment is strongly influenced by the reactions of others. If the action is punished, it is bad; if it is rewarded, it is good. This practice stems from the child's total acceptance of adults as sources of rules and rewards. Evidence shows, however, that this evaluation does break down if responses are vastly out of line with the reaction the child has come to expect. Thus, children who have been lured into incestuous actions by a trusted adult tend to be able to recognize the activity as wrong, even though the adult assures them it is all right.

Fourth, the young child does not think of the cooperative benefits in behavior toward others. The child does not seek to elicit kindness from others by being kind to them. The child is only focused on how the other person behaved first. The child does not see his or her own behavior toward others as significant in influencing personal actions. Thus, a two-year-old who hits another child is surprised if that child retaliates. The connection between the two hits is simply not recognized.

Fifth, young children view punishment as a necessary balance for wrongdoing. However, they give no thought to actual restitution. A spanking or similar punishment seems to elicit a sense of relief, for it removes the feelings of guilt. The child rarely thinks of some kind of effort to undo the damage. Nor is the child usually interested in the idea if it is suggested.

The *sixth* aspect of immature moral judgment is a tendency to view misfortune as the natural outcome of some previous misbehavior. Three- and four-year-olds often view inanimate objects as transmitters of deserved punishment. Thus, a child sees falling down as the expected outcome of disobedience. The ground conspires to make it happen. Much of this thinking may be the result of such parental admonitions as, "Don't come crying to me! I warned you not to do that. You just got what you deserved."[12] [13]

Because of the limitations of childish thought, attempts that require a child to verbally express adult (or even biblical) moral views succeed at only a superficial level. For example, having a child memorize a relevant Bible verse ("Be kind...to one another" [Eph. 4:32]) tends to cause the child to view the verse as another rule to be followed, rather than as explaining why such behavior is desirable. Adults who are concerned about developing Christian ethics in the young child need to focus their attentions primarily on the kind of models they are providing for childish imitation. Because action precedes language with the young child, strictly verbal attempts to guide moral growth are generally ineffective during the preschool years, and of only limited value in the elementary years.

Activities for Learning About People

Learning About Adults

Nothing helps a child learn how to relate to people more effectively than providing meaningful interaction with understanding and loving adults. The Bible consistently identifies parents as the adults who have this responsibility. The child loves others only as he or she has been loved. The child respects the rights of family members in accord with the respect he or she has received. The child seeks to share and help as he or she has been helped. Parents who claim they have given a child everything often omit the most essential factor for helping the child learn how to live a purposeful life—themselves.

Many parents unknowingly, yet skillfully, teach their children negative ways of behaving through consistent patterns of emotional neglect. Kim's situation was sadly typical. Her mother ignored Kim's attempts to get her attention. Kim kept trying to gain a response. Each attempt was louder than the last. By the time her mother did respond, both were irritated. Communication that could have been enjoyable for both became an ordeal. As this pattern was unintentionally repeated, Kim developed negative feelings about herself and her mother, not because her mother did not love her, but because she did not understand the way her child needed that love to be expressed.

Teachers must also recognize a child's deep longing to be valued.

Group learning situations require personal attention for each child. Young children tend to look upon the teacher as the mommy or daddy of the room. One reason many parents opt to home-school their children is the often valid fear that the classroom teacher will simply not have the time, energy and/or interest in giving each child the needed personal attention. The teacher who builds a personal relationship with a child, however, soon becomes a model for the child's behavior. When the teacher shares similar values as the parents, the cooperative influence of both home and classroom is very powerful. When the teacher adheres to different or opposing values, parents still have the inside track in influencing the child as long as they consistently invest significant amounts of time, energy and emotion to maintain a supportive relationship on which the child can depend.

In addition to parents and teachers, children need contact with many other adults. It is important to assist the child in viewing neighbors, postal workers, store clerks, librarians and others as friendly helpers. Within the Christian community, pastors, missionaries and other church workers can help in the child's growing understanding of adults, to the degree the child is allowed personal contact with them. Concerned parents need to consider carefully the people they want to have become significant parts of their child's life, then plan ways to include those people in the child's activities. Whether choosing day care, forming a play group, selecting playmates or registering for soccer, the decision must always involve more than just schedule, location and transportation, though these are major factors in every busy parent's life. High priority must always be given to "who"—the people who become part of a child's expanded relationships.

Learning About Peers

Associations with other children of similar ages are essential for developing a child's interpersonal attitudes and skills. Although young children are intensely interested in other young children, they do not always find it easy to develop friendships. Often, other children are seen as potential threats to a child's domain.

Jesus clearly made loving behavior toward others a cornerstone of the Christian faith. "Love your neighbor as yourself" (Matt. 22:39) is the second greatest of all God's commandments. "A new command I give you: Love one another" (John 13:34), Jesus told His disciples.

The child becomes capable of loving by first receiving love and by learning to interact positively with other people. Love is never experienced in the abstract or at a long distance. It is always a personal, intimate experience. The growing child needs a foundation of positive interactions with other children as a basis for being able to show loving actions and attitudes. A Sunday School that talks and sings about loving one another and being kind friends, but provides little or no opportunity for children to talk with each other, is a classic case of contradictions.

As the child experiences the ups and downs, the give and take of playing with others, some of the most important lessons of life are learned. Sensitive adults can help the child in this process by providing appropriate equipment, adequate space and just enough supervision to keep everyone safe and involved.

For children who are not yet secure enough to share a toy, having duplicates of the popular pieces of equipment can ease feelings of uncertainty. Also, many games can help lay a foundation for enjoyable sharing.

- Variations of "peekaboo," the all-time favorite for one-year-olds, can help a little one still enjoy a toy, even though it is not in his or her immediate possession. Hide a favorite toy from view (under a towel). Wait a moment, then remove the towel with a flourish. The demand for many repetitions of this feat is evidence that the child is learning that surrendering a toy can sometimes be more fun than holding on to it.
- Rolling a ball back and forth with a two-year-old is another way of developing good feelings about sharing. Both the enjoyment of making the ball roll and the anticipation of its return are more fun than just standing around and holding on to the ball. Including another child in the game adds to the fun. "Jon and Bobby are good friends. I thank God for good friends."
- Three-year-olds love "hide-and-seek," as long as the hiding places are fairly obvious. The fun is in the finding, not in the seeking. The greatest asset is that hide-and-seek requires at least two to play.
- Any activity that involves taking turns helps to build positive feelings toward other children.

Playing house and building with blocks are absorbing activities for four- and five-year-olds. Conflicts will arise, of course, but the desire for a playmate is strong enough that children generally exert the necessary efforts to overcome problems. The result is a valuable learning experience. Adult reinforcement of desired behavior adds greatly to the likelihood of that behavior reoccurring. A few clearly defined rules help to minimize problems:

- "You can knock down your own building. Only (Angela) can knock down her tower."
- "You can build as high as your shoulders."
- "Build only on this side of the tape (a strip placed two to three feet in front of the block shelf). That leaves room for others to get some blocks to use."

Some children need special help in learning how to play with other children. It is difficult to show love when the child is unable to communicate. Sometimes in busy classrooms or playgrounds where a great deal of activity is occurring, teachers miss noticing that some children always play alone, even when surrounded by others. Although solitary play can be satisfying to a child at times, it can be highly demoralizing when it results not from choice, but from the lack of an ability to relate.

One approach to helping the solitary child is to promote activities that require cooperation. Teeter-totter, sandboxes, block building and water play are activities that are more fun for two children than for one. Identify the good feelings with words. "David, you and Rosie are really playing well together. You are kind friends. The Bible says, 'Be kind to...one another.'" Some children, however, will rigorously avoid these activities rather than face the specter of failure in personal relationships.

This situation can often be helped by giving the lonely child access to an attractive activity with the hope of drawing other children to interact in it. One teacher offered a child who had difficulty relating to others the opportunity to paint a piece of playground equipment. The child responded enthusiastically. As he began to work, the teacher said, "Some other children might come over and say they want to paint, too. What will you tell them?" He had no answer.

She then offered several possible responses he could make, from "No!" to "Yes, but you will have to get a brush out of the cabinet." After each suggestion she helped the child predict how the other child might respond. Then she withdrew and watched as gradually the other children began to approach him. The confidence he felt from controlling the activity helped him to initiate several brief conversations. He also responded to questions asked by the other children.

Notice that the teacher not only arranged an activity in which the lonely boy would be the center of attention, but she also provided him with specific conversation ideas to help him take advantage of the situation. It is common for children, as well as adults, to retreat into silence or to resort to unproductive physical efforts, simply because they do not have the right words to use.

Avoid comparing one child with another or fostering competition among young children. Children can be helped, however, by learning from what other children do. Often a child will hold back from a new experience until observing the behavior of other children. The child may then try it. Commending children in the presence of other children is helpful, if rigorous care is taken to be sure every child receives the praise he or she needs. Usually the least capable child needs the most recognition, but often receives the least.

Statements such as the following give recognition to children. They also focus the attention of others on the desired behavior, but do not make some children feel less worthy than others.

- "Carlos is showing me that he is ready for our story. He is sitting flat on the rug with his hands in his lap. Andrea is ready, too, and so is David."
- "I would like to put your finger painting up on the wall with the others so that everyone can see the many different ways that the children made designs."
- "Everyone who is wearing something green may stand up quietly and tiptoe to the door."
- "If you know the answer to my question, put your hand on your head. Good! Rachel knows. Hillary knows. Daniel has his hand on his head. Marvin, tell me the answer." (Avoid the habit of always calling on the first child who responds. The above conversation allows many children to be affirmed, and allows the teacher to select the child who will give the answer aloud.)

- "Jeff did something the Bible talks about. The Bible says to share what you have, and Jeff gave some of his play dough to Amy."
- "I'm thinking of someone in our class who (has a ribbon in her hair, wears glasses just like I do, used a lot of red in a painting this morning, and so on)." Then invite children to give a clue describing someone in the group.

Children can become more aware of others as individuals by hearing the names of other children, as well as their own. For instance, encourage children to draw pictures to send to a specific child who is absent. "Kevin will be very glad to get this picture from his friends. God planned for us to have friends."

One enterprising teacher made up booklets for her kindergartners. On the front of each booklet she lettered the title "My Friends." Each child was encouraged to ask his or her friends to do something on one page in the book, such as write their names, draw a picture, outline their hands or place a thumbprint. The booklet served as a device to encourage children to think about their friends and to interact with other children. The teacher watched for opportunities in which she could call the children's attention to God's plan that they love and enjoy their friends. "How glad we are for our friends at church! Thank You, God, for good friends who love us."

Appreciation of individual differences is significant in helping a child acquire a wholesome attitude toward others. Developing perceptual skills through such activities as those mentioned in the "Activities for Learning About Things" section of this chapter can play a major role in developing a child's awareness of another child's uniqueness. Observing the multitudinous differences in plant and animal life can also help a child enjoy the differences that are part of human experiences.

Interaction with children and adults in various settings provides many opportunities to experience these differences. As adults accept and enjoy these differences in age, sex, race, ability and interest, the child will follow this lead. Unfortunately, prejudice and bigotry will also be communicated in the same way. Overriding all other factors, the attitude and behavior of parents and teachers provide a pattern that will either help or hinder the child in developing a healthy view of God's world and the people He has made for it.

Notes

1. David Elkind, *Understanding Your Child from Birth to Sixteen* (Boston: Allyn and Bacon, 1994), p. 5.
2. Howard Gardner, *The Unschooled Mind* (New York: Basic Books, 1991), p. 45.
3. Jean Piaget, *The Construction of Reality in the Child* (New York: Basic Books, 1954), pp. 76-80.
4. Gardner, *The Unschooled Mind*, p. 48.
5. Ronald Goldman, *Religious Thinking from Childhood to Adolescence* (New York: Seabury Press, 1964), p. 95.
6. Jean Piaget, *The Child's Conception of the World* (Lanham, Md.: Littlefield, 1975), p. 376.
7. Ibid., pp. 258-259
8. M. O. Nelson, "The Concept of God and the Feelings Toward Parents," *Journal of Individual Psychology* 27 (1971): 44-52.
9. P. Brown and R. Elliott, "Control of Aggression in a Nursery School Class," *Journal of Experimental Child Psychology* 2 (1965): 13-107.
10. P. H. Whiteman and K. P. Kosier, "Development of Children's Moralistic Judgments," *Child Development* 35 (1964): 843-850.
11. R. Selman, "Taking Another's Perspective," *Child Development* 42 (1971): 1721-1734.
12. Jean Piaget, *The Moral Judgment of the Child* (Glencoe, Ill.: Free Press, 1948).
13. Lawrence Kohlberg, "Development of Moral Character and Moral Ideology," in *Review of Child Development Research*, vol. 1, eds. M. Hoffman and L. Hoffman (New York: Russell Sage Foundation, 1964), pp. 396 ff.

C H A P T E R

4

The Child and the Church

I rejoiced with those who said to me, "Let us go to the house of the Lord."
—Psalm 122:1

"Is this really God's house?"
"Why do you ask, Jimmy?"
"Well, when I come here He's never home."

Jimmy's question is very natural for a five-year-old who understands and uses words in their most literal sense. Derek had a similar reaction when told he was in God's house. "Where's His bedroom?" he asked.

Church from a Child's Perspective

To the child, the church building can be an intriguing and somewhat mysterious place. Church is constantly associated with God. From such phrases as "the house of the Lord," the child concludes that the church is the physical dwelling of God. When also told that God lives in heaven, confusion results. Although such misunderstandings can usually be explained to the child's satisfaction, it is clear that children, especially when younger than six years old, have a limited understanding of what the church really is.

The child brings the same thought process to bear on understanding the church as with any other matter. For example, the child's viewpoint is dominated by impressions from often irrelevant factors. Young children frequently express the uniqueness of the church in terms of some physical feature of the building, such as a towering spire, colored windows, rows of chairs or big doors.

Some children focus on special ceremonies they have witnessed, such as weddings, funerals or baptisms, as the most important function of the church. Robes, backward collars and big books are often vivid in the child's thinking as being essential to the church's operations. Even less obvious physical features and specific incidents can dominate childish thought about what the church is.[1] Four-year-old Jennie protested that an outdoor worship service "really isn't church 'cause I don't have on my white shoes." The young child is likely to fasten attention on some nonessential factor, convinced that is what the church is all about.

Why We Go to Church

The young child has very little insight into the purpose for going to church. Specific actions such as listening to stories, singing songs, holding the Bible, painting pictures and eating crackers are just a few of the motives commonly expressed. "Because it's Sunday," "So Daddy can sleep" and "To make God happy" are some four-year-olds' explanations for church attendance. A child gives these kinds of answers in all seriousness, assured that they explain adequately the real purpose in it all.

Even the child who can give "right" answers, such as "To learn about God," "To worship God" or "To study the Bible," usually has no adequate conception of what these words really mean. Further questioning quickly shows those answers are often a mere recitation of statements heard from adults. Even through the elementary years, most children remain blissfully vague about the purpose of going to church in spite of extensive efforts by parents and teachers to explain.

Underlying many answers is the child's vague feeling that church attendance is some kind of trade agreement with God, obligating Him to bestow special favors. Or, from the negative side, it is a means to avoid God's displeasure. Much of the reason for this lack of understanding is that the question simply is not a burning issue for the child.

Although the child may have positive or negative feelings about what happens when at church, attending or not attending is not really a decision the child must make. The adults in the child's life usually decide if the child will attend. They notify the child of the proper day and time and take care of transportation there and back. The child may be happy or unhappy with the decision, but the purpose of it all is not a practical issue the child must resolve. In situations where a child is the one who makes the choice, the reason for attending may be more related to being with friends, liking a teacher or having a good time than because of any identifiable religious understanding.

These vague ideas about the reason for attending church also show in the child's awareness of religious identity. Although many five- to seven-year-olds may be able to proclaim that they are Baptists, Catholics or Nazarenes, the significance of the label totally escapes them. Such designations are often confused with national or ethnic distinctions (i.e., "I'm not a Baptist. I'm American!"). Through the elementary years, children gradually come to understand at least the major features that distinguish their denomination or group from others.[2]

What We Do at Church

The meaning of specific acts of worship is difficult for a child to grasp. Because the child thinks literally, the symbolism of church sacraments and ceremonies often results in superficial understandings. The physical aspects of the Lord's Supper and baptism, for example, dominate the child's thinking, often to the exclusion of the intended meaning of the symbols. Such misunderstanding occurs even when the child may be able to use the "correct" verbal labels.

"When my mommy gives me a bath she takes my clothes off," was Angie's declaration upon observing her first water baptismal service. The physical properties of this sacrament also tend to dominate the young child's thinking to the exclusion of the symbolic meaning of the act. Exposure to these dramatic portrayals does raise questions for the child. The answers adults give need to be phrased simply, using words the child understands. One thoughtful parent explained the observance of the Lord's Supper: "Jesus tells us in the Bible to have this special time so we will remember how very much He loves us."

Offerings greatly intrigue a young child. Five-year-old Gordon surprised his parents one Sunday when he announced proudly that Jesus had been in his Sunday School room. Pursuing the matter a little further, they found that the usher who came into the room to pick up the offering container was Gordon's idea of Jesus. Gordon's teachers had carefully explained that the children were giving their money to Jesus. And in Gordon's literal thinking, what could be a more logical conclusion! Gordon and his friends needed a more specific and definite explanation of what happens to offering money.

Also, because young children are usually not giving something of their own, but are merely transporting coins given to them for this purpose, giving an offering has only limited value in their learning to share. Attempting to build such a habit in a child before the child has either understanding or ability to choose is neither educationally sound nor biblically accurate. Parents and teachers need to explain in simple terms that "we bring money because we love God and other people." Also, showing the child items (Bibles, storybooks, materials and equipment) that offering money buys helps to clarify this concept. Once children are given or earn some money of their own to spend, encouraging them to give an offering becomes valid.

How We Behave at Church

Children's presence in the church's worship service is often intended by parents to teach their children to worship and to sit still in church. This latter concern stems partly from the parents' desire for the child not to disturb either the parents or other adults during the service. Frequently, parents hold the conviction that this "training" of a young child is necessary if the child is to behave properly in church services when older. A certain degree of restlessness and noise may be tolerated as cute when the child is 3 years old. Parents fearfully ask, however, "But what if she acts like that in church when she's 13 years old?"

Requiring a child to sit quietly for an hour or more during a program having little or no features planned to attract the child's interest is a tall order. Thus, some parents resort to threats, bribes or some quiet form of entertainment, or hope the child will go to sleep. Some children settle in fairly comfortably, enjoying being with the grown-ups and keeping disturbance to a minimum. Success in getting a child to sit still, however, is not an indicator that the child has been introduced to worship experiences in a meaningful way.

Keeping even the most active child quiet is never difficult when the child finds something of captivating interest. Even one- and two-year-olds can remain involved for extended time periods in an activity in which they are interested and involved. Rather than wrestling with a child who has too much energy to sit still in church, parents could more wisely use their energies in helping the church plan a program designed to capture the interest of the child.

In general, it is better for a child to spend the worship service time in a program designed to meet a child's special needs, rather than to endure an adult meeting where little or nothing is planned with a child's understandings and interest in mind. As each child grows, his or her attention span will lengthen. The time will come when the matters being talked and sung about in an adult worship service will have real appeal, for they will deal with recognizable needs and concerns. That time, however, is not during the years of early childhood. In a great many churches, depending to a large extent on the style and length of the service, most children do not begin to understand and consistently participate in worship experiences until adolescence.

How, then, does a child learn to sit still in church? The child learns mostly by growing older and allowing his or her nervous system to mature. Imposing inactivity on a child whose whole being demands activity is unlikely to make a child think that church is a good place to be. As little Timmy put it when told that God would not like his noise: "Doesn't God like little boys?"

One of the problems in helping children develop reverence is the example set by adults. Not that children see adults running in the halls, yelling over crowds or throwing paper airplanes in the foyer. Children, however, do see adults in the church building doing all of the normal things they see adults doing elsewhere: standing around, talking with friends, laughing and often drinking coffee. To the child, adult behavior in and near the church buildings does not appear to differ from adult behavior at home, the store or any other public place. Why, then, should children's behavior be expected to differ from the normal activities of children at home or school? Adults often do an effective job of confusing children by employing this subtle double standard, using pious declarations as their rationale for banning certain actions by the child.

Christians who want children to grow up within the family of the church should make sure the church can accept children as they are, not as adults wish they were or hope they will become. This does not mean children are allowed to run amok. It does mean children deserve to be respected as real people—people having value because of who they are today—not just because someday they may grow up and become important.

How We Feel About Church

Although the young child's understanding of the church is limited, and childlike behavior often seems out of place, even the infant and toddler are immensely capable of forming strong feelings about the church and their experiences there. In an interesting survey on this subject, Dr. Ronald Goldman questioned several hundred English children. He discovered that their attitudes toward the church had little to do with their own patterns of attendance. Rather, the single most powerful influence on the child's feelings about church evolved from whether the parents attended church.[3] Parental interests have such a strong effect on the child that their attitudes actually are dominant over the child's own experience.

Those parents for whom church attendance is a meaningful part of life transmit their feelings to the child. The child is thus prepared for what then becomes a far more positive experience than would occur if parental enthusiasm had not existed. When parents show by their words and their manner that they enjoy church participation, the child, seeking to be like them, will imitate their attitudes and actions. When parents display negative attitudes concerning church involvement, this attitude will likely diminish whatever enjoyments the child discovers.

A child's experiences at church, however, cannot be discounted as unimportant. Positive, pleasant experiences make a major contribution to a child's concept of church, just as negative encounters can build resistance. The child forms impressions, not from verbal statements explaining the church, but from the real church the child attends. Both parents and teachers share the responsibility for providing a situation at church that expresses to a child, "Welcome! This place is for you!"

The appearance of the rooms, the preparation of the teachers and the materials that are available to use all convey a sense that church has been planned to help the child learn of God in the way children learn best—by doing. To help a child feel good about church attendance, allow ample participation in activities appropriate to the child's age-level interests, building stable and meaningful relationships with teachers and other children, all mingled with enjoyable moments of spontaneous worship.

If a church could accomplish only one thing with a child through the early years of life, it should seek to help the child feel loved by the people at church. The child who looks at the church building and thinks *The people here love me,* has a solid foundation on which to discover the church as more than a building, but as a group of people who love God and love each other.

Activities for Learning About Church

Attendance
The most effective way parents can stimulate a child's interest in church is to attend regularly themselves. Parental example plays a key role in strengthening the child's feelings about church attendance. Similarly, teachers who are consistent in their attendance show the importance of the church in their lives.

Conversation
Conversations with the child concerning experiences at church help reinforce what the child has experienced, conveying a sense of the importance of church to parents and teachers. Rather than simply asking, "What did you learn at church today?" parents can enrich the child's time at church by using thoughtful comments and questions. A few examples:

- "Sing one of your Sunday School songs for me."
- "Let's talk about what we liked best about church this morning. Do you want to talk first or second?"
- "Tell me something about the story your teacher told you today."
- "Hum part of one of the songs you sang and see if I can guess what some of the words are."

- "Tell me the first name (or initial) of three people you talked to at church. I'll try to guess who they were."
- "Who can be the first one to think of something you learned today that you didn't know before (or that you had forgotten about)?"

Focusing on a specific part of the child's experience rather than on general topics helps a child recall particular events. When the child brings home a picture drawn or painted in church school, suggest, "Tell me something about this picture." Casual conversations about these things encourage the child to talk about experiences, often giving an adult an opportunity to correct misconceptions.

Use the Sunday School curriculum resources provided by your church to initiate activities that expand on your child's learning at church. A meeting of parents and teachers to discuss such activities as songs, finger fun (poems with finger/hand motions, such as "This is the church, this is the steeple, open the door, and where's all the people?") and creative art can also be helpful. Because most children are not consciously aware of learning (they assume they already know everything), casual conversations about what went on are helpful in stimulating thought and interest.

Adult Worship Visits

Children are naturally interested in whatever interests adults, so occasional visits to adult worship services can help widen a child's understanding. This is especially true if parents or teachers talk with the child ahead of time in preparation for what the child will see and hear. Teachers should consult the pastor for a suitable time in which a group of children can visit—such as during the beginning moments of the service, or at a time when no service is being held. Perhaps the pastor can meet briefly with the children before or after their visit.

Before a child attends adult worship, it is helpful to visit the room in advance, walking with the child to get a close-up view of specific features that are likely to attract a child's attention (pulpit, large Bible, organ or other musical instruments, colorful windows, altar railing, offering plates and so on).

When arriving for the service itself, make sure that the child is included in any welcoming conversations with greeters, ushers and others attending worship. If a printed bulletin contains the order of worship, point out a few parts of the service that may be of greatest interest to the child.

Sit where the child has a clear, uninterrupted view of the pulpit area. In most cases, the closer toward the front, the better, because a child sitting toward the back is less likely to listen to what is being said from the front. As certain people participate in the various parts of the service, whisper to the child who each one is, and something of interest about that person. ("That tall usher with the blue jacket is Mr. Mendez. He's the manager at our grocery store.") If the child gets restless, be ready to slip out quietly and spend a few moments talking about what occurred during the service.

If you make such a visit when no service is in progress, direct a child's attention to any unique features he or she may notice. Sit quietly with a child for a few moments to sense the beauty and quietness. Encourage the child to carefully examine hymnals, Bibles or bulletins that are used during worship. Ask simple questions to help a child see any colors and designs in windows or banners.

On the way to (or from) the sanctuary, walk past the church sign. Guide the children in naming letters in the words on the sign. Then let the child help you "read" the sign. Take a picture of the child or group outside the church building. Also, direct attention to any distinctive feature, such as a cross or spire, that marks your church building. Explain, "This cross helps people know this is a church building—a special place to come to learn of God and the Lord Jesus."

You may want to plan more than one excursion to examine the various things of interest throughout your church building. Also, teachers may want to plan for several small groups of children to tour, one group at a time, rather than as one larger group. When children return from their tour, ask simple questions to help children recall their experience. However such visits are conducted, they are best when kept brief and treated as special occasions.

A tour of the church building is most appropriate when a class is studying about the church. The most important part of the church for a young child, however, is *his* or *her* own room and the teachers who are there.

Children's Worship Program
Several basic things should characterize a program at church designed for children. These factors should be built into the Sunday School,

Children's Church, Sunday-evening service or anytime children are at church.

Child focus. First, design the schedule and the content based on a child's needs and interests. A child needs involvement with firsthand experiences far more than the secondhand experience of listening to an adult talk. Avoid the tendency to pattern the children's program after what the adults are doing. The best preparation for later stages of growth is to fully meet the needs and interests of the current stage.

Relationships. Second, involve understanding and patient adults who sincerely care for each child. Personal attention from sensitive adults, and pleasant interaction with other children, add the human element that is essential to Christian nurturing and development. These adults become visible representations to the child of what God is like— an awesome but thrilling responsibility.

Facilities. Third, provide ample space and materials for a variety of active learning experiences, allowing children to learn in the ways that are most efficient for them. For example, a room for young children should provide home-living experiences, blocks for building, living plants and/or animals to observe, puzzles, creative art, children's books and music. These ingredients of a good program for young children may not be available every week, but there should be enough variety to let children choose from several options.

Music. Words set to rhythmic patterns and melody are the easiest form of verbal communication for children to remember. Music at church is a powerful means for enjoyable and repeated learning. A child's enjoyment of a song grows by having repeated opportunities to hear and sing it. Seeing pictures and objects that illustrate the words helps to increase interest and learning. Because of the influence of words set to music, the songs that are sung at church need to be carefully selected to accommodate the understanding of the child. Symbolism and advanced vocabulary should be avoided, choosing songs with words that clearly and simply say exactly what they mean.

The words should also express feelings and thoughts with which the child can easily identify. Singing these songs at home, as well as at church, provides parents with a valuable way to strengthen the bridge between church and home. Learning the songs the child likes to sing at church is an effective way to show that what the child does at church is important to parents. And the nice thing about singing with young children is that no matter whether the adult may drift off-key, it doesn't matter to the child! It's the adult's enthusiasm that sparks the child's interest.

Worship. A variety of things tend to get labeled as "worship" in church circles. Although adults tend to envision worship as fairly structured experiences, the most meaningful worship for children often occurs at spontaneous moments. Pausing for a moment of awe and wonder to breathe a quick prayer of gratitude is an effective way for an adult to lead a child in thankfulness to God.

When the child is wide-eyed about the colors of a butterfly wing, the teacher can express his or her own feelings of reverence, providing a model for the child to follow. Pausing for a few seconds of gratitude is an effective way for an adult to lead a child in expressing thankfulness to God. Or, pausing to pray about a problem that has just been raised is a powerful means of involving a child, not just in learning *about* worship, but in learning *to* worship. The moments of interest and wonder that come through the child's discoveries are usually far more meaningful than the routine forms of worship in adult settings far beyond the child's level of understanding.

Most important of all, the effect of the child's experiences at church depends on the quality of the relationships with people there. The church that is concerned that its children feel loved must provide understanding and patient adults who sincerely love each child. Personal attention from sensitive adults, in addition to pleasant interaction with other children, add the human element that is essential to Christian nurture and development. These adults also become visible representations to the child of what God is like—an awesome but thrilling responsibility for all those who guide young children.

Notes

1. Ronald Goldman, *Religious Thinking from Childhood to Adolescence* (New York: Seabury Press, 1964), p. 199.
2. David Elkind, *Understanding Your Child from Birth to Sixteen* (Boston: Allyn and Bacon, 1994), p. 150.
3. Goldman, *Religious Thinking from Childhood to Adolescence*, p. 194.

C H A P T E R

5

The Child, the Bible and Prayer

*I seek you with all my heart; do not let me stray
from your commands.*
—Psalm 119:10

"I don't think I like God."

"Why?"

"Because it says she (the 'I' of Psalm 23) doesn't want Him."

"Oh, that means He won't let the person want for anything he needs."

"But He makes her lie down on the ground."

"You would like that if you were a sheep."

"I don't want to be a sheep."

This five-year-old had earned the praise and admiration of her parents and teachers for memorizing Psalm 23. Her performance had been all that adults could ask of a child's recitation, spoken with every evidence of assurance and understanding. And then, almost as an afterthought, she said, "I don't think I like God." She had succeeded from all outward appearances, but the sense she made of the Scripture passage was something totally different from what the adults assumed.

The Bible and prayer are aspects of Christian life the child can experience directly. Yet, they are often shrouded with intrigue and mystery, as well as misunderstanding. The child is told that through the Bible God speaks directly to him or her, and through prayer the child can personally address God. As in the case of the little girl and Psalm 23, understanding these concepts presents difficulties for the child's developing thought processes.

The Child and the Bible

Children easily develop positive feelings about the Bible, although they understand very little of it.[1] Children are told the Bible is important, and they accept the judgment of the adults in their lives. Symbolic terms, however, such as "lamp," "sword" and "bread," made in reference to the Bible, misguide a child's literal thinking. Older children are also easily confused unless they are given clear explanations. Often a child selects some nonessential factor as the Bible's distinguishing mark. The Bible's physical appearance, its age, its adult language and its use in church may seem to a child to be the unique quality that makes it such a significant book. The child has little or no comprehension of its construction, other than a vague notion that God wrote it. Because it is the vehicle through which Christian concepts are communicated to the child, any misconceptions about the Bible can affect many other concepts and feelings.

One problem in using the Bible with young children grows out of efforts to teach the child about the Bible as an isolated subject. Adults often seem compelled to impress a child with the importance of certain information. ("You need to pay close attention because this story teaches us a very important lesson God wants us to know.") Thus, Bible stories and statements are often prefaced with comments to make the child take special note of what is being said. In most cases, it would probably be just as effective to merely state that the incident really happened, and let the Bible story stand on its own merits. To do more than that often clouds the issue by making the people and events seem so unique that the child cannot identify with them and tends to assume they were different from "real" people the child knows.

For example, a kindergarten teacher had just returned from a trip to Israel. She wanted to help the children visualize the scenes where many of the Bible stories occurred. So she displayed photographs she had taken in Israel. Much to her surprise, the most interesting fact for the children was simply the idea that she had been able to physically go to those locations. Many of the children found it hard to believe that the Bible stories had occurred at real places. As one little boy put it, "You can't go to Bethlehem. It's in heaven." The teacher's efforts to impress the children with the Bible's sacred character had removed the stories from the children's understanding of physical reality.

Historical-Cultural Gap

A major barrier to the child understanding the Bible is the immense historical and cultural gap that exists between the limited experience of the modern child and the events of biblical narrative. For example, most children under the age of six have difficulty recalling recent events from their own experiences. Asking them to develop accurate mental pictures of biblical events is a tall order. The child, whose thought patterns naturally center on self, assumes that everyone else lives similarly. This mind-set is hard to shake because the young child is convinced others view all situations with the same perspective. Sometimes attempts to explain some of the critical differences in modes of living, acting and thinking only add to the problem, for the child is likely to twist the information to fit a child's-eye view of life.

For example, many Bible stories that take place around a well lose much of their significance to a child who cannot visualize an alternative to modern plumbing. Also, most families of the Bible may seem somewhat unreal to the child whose entire family experience is restricted to a common pattern of fewer children, working mothers and, often, absent fathers. The sacrificial worship at the Tabernacle or Temple is totally foreign to the background of today's child. And what impression or lesson does a four-year-old receive from the Old Testament battle narratives?

Compounding the culture separation is the inability of the child to understand the sequence of time. For the child who gathers all past memories under the vague umbrella term of "yesterday" or "last night," the scope of biblical chronology is hopelessly complex. The child who is dominated by the present and has only dim awareness of the years since babyhood finds it difficult to think of Jesus as infant, boy and man. The little boy who envisioned baby Moses leading the Israelites across the Red Sea in baskets woven by their mothers was using all his mental powers to make all his pieces of information fit. Even into the older elementary years, children find it difficult to understand which characters and events came before or after Jesus, let alone the vast differences in customs, values and worship patterns in various periods of biblical history.

Vocabulary

Another difficulty for the child is the vocabulary of the Bible. Biblical names, for example, often make the characters appear strange to the child. Also, the archaic wording of the *King James* Bible English tends to make people and events obscure. Many words that are essential to biblical narrative and meaning often are grossly misunderstood by a child.

A teacher was telling her group of five-year-olds the story of the good Samaritan. To encourage participation, she asked if they knew what "robbers" were. Every hand went up, for they had all heard the term many times on television. But not one child could tell what a robber does. The teacher was startled, for "robbers" was hardly one of the more difficult words in the story. Yet, none of the children understood the term. Thus, they missed much of the story's meaning.

Such misunderstandings lead to another problem—the facility with which children can seem to understand and yet miss the whole point. Mere survival in a world beyond their abilities to comprehend seems to force the child into developing the skill of acting as though everything is understood even when it is not. Group singing illustrates this point. Each child may appear to be contributing with gusto to what sounds like a well-vocalized piece of music. Isolation of any one singer, however, often produces a strange outpouring of sense and nonsense. A child who does not know the words simply fills in with noise that sounds like what everyone else is singing. The amazing thing is that the child sings the gibberish with the same confidence as the words, totally oblivious to any lack of meaning.

In the area of Christian concepts, this misunderstanding is a serious problem. The child, unable to understand the meaning of a word, phrase or idea, is often unaware of any error, and answers by repeating words adults or another child have used. Parents and teachers show pleasure at hearing the child mouth the proper arrangement of words. They seldom press further to discover what meaning those words really possess for the child.

Memorization

Rote memorization also can compound the child's difficulty in understanding Scripture. Zealous adults often strive to have a child commit to memory something "you will understand later on." Or, they merely assume the child understands because for them the meaning is obvious.

So the child says the words. The proud adults beam. The child, however, may have no adequate understanding. Words, phrases and ideas
that are unrelated to the child's present experience have little or no
immediate or long-range significance for the child.[2]

The effort expended on recitation could be far more profitably
expended on activities (such as those suggested in the "Activities for
Learning About the Bible" and "Activities for Learning About Prayer"
sections of this chapter) where biblical statements are used in direct
relation to the activity in which the child is presently engaged or has
recently experienced.

Symbolism

Symbolism presents another difficulty in a child's understanding Bible
content. Many biblical concepts are expressed through imagery and
allegories that have great importance for adults, but produce confusion
for the child whose thinking is dominated by the literal meanings of
words. For example, the child who has a still developing self-concept
will find the idea of being a sheep or a branch as most unpleasant, often
truly unthinkable. Although a child may enjoy pretending to be something else, the fun is in recognizing that it is only make-believe. Serious
concepts presented symbolically are usually taken seriously, which for
the child means literally.

The child's great difficulty in handling symbolism means that rarely,
if ever, can a child think beyond the literal symbol to perceive the rich
meaning it is intended to portray.[3] Because the Bible frequently uses
symbolism to convey ideas, the child faces a great problem in understanding. But again, this is a problem the child does not know exists.

For example, many of Jesus' parables—superb examples of teaching
through symbolism—are misunderstood by children. Although they
may enjoy hearing about the lost sheep, the lost coin, the mustard seed,
or the sower and the seed, they tend to view them as merely interesting
stories about sheep, coins and seeds. The ability to see themselves in the
word pictures Jesus drew has just not developed yet.

Efforts to use these kinds of stories to apply truth to the life experiences of children prove very difficult. Older children also have problems
taking an idea from one setting and using it in another situation. The
straightforward narrative of the parable of the good Samaritan, which
clearly illustrates one person helping another person in need, is fre-

quently misinterpreted by 11- and 12-year-olds when asked to apply its teaching to another set of circumstances.[4] How much more difficult is this task with children under 6 years of age?

Miracles

The Bible's miracles often pose a unique difficulty for the young child's comprehension. The problem is not one of belief, for the young child readily accepts the miraculous. The problem is one of practice. For example, a Sunday School teacher was telling her four-year-olds about some children who were very disappointed because a promised picnic had been rained out. She asked her class what those children could possibly do that would be better than fussing about this setback. The unanimous conclusion was that the children should pray, asking God to stop the rain. And one little boy added, "Just like Jesus did in the boat."

The child thinks logically, *Because God loves me and has all that power, He should be willing to use it to solve my problem.* And because the child is convinced that nothing is more important than the immediate present, obviously, God should feel the same way. The young child tends to view the miraculous as expected everyday occurrences, because cause-and-effect relationships are still so imperfectly understood at that young age. The operation of an automobile engine is as much a mystery as the parting of the Red Sea. The child thus has a difficult time drawing a workable line between the natural and the supernatural. A child who hears a story of a biblical miracle accepts it uncritically along with all the other remarkable things in the world that seem to happen so amazingly.

Perhaps the most important thing for a child to understand about a Bible story involving a miracle is the purpose for God's action. Stories of a physical healing, for example, can be used effectively to show Jesus' love for a person. "Jesus helped the blind man to see because He loved him" is a logical and meaningful explanation a child can grasp.

"Jesus loved His friends. Jesus didn't want His friends to be afraid. He helped them by stopping the storm." This emphasis focuses the child's attention on Jesus' deed, not as an end in itself, but as an example of showing love and compassion to friends in need.

The Significance of These Difficulties

It is difficult to measure the effect on the child of these difficulties in understanding biblical content. It is presumptuous to expect a beginning student in any subject to start out by having a mature concept of that subject. To find a childish misconception about a Bible story is no more surprising than to find childish errors in spelling and arithmetic. These errors are actually key building blocks in the learning process. As errors become evident, patient and loving adults can guide the child in ways that will help clarify an understanding of Bible truths.

This process of correcting misconceptions, however, does not often happen in dealing with the Bible. Adults tend to assume that the child's ability to remember Bible story facts indicates that the child adequately understands the significance of the story. Thus, the child is allowed to continue assuming knowledge of what a given story is all about, when in fact the point may be totally missed.

Many such evidences are seen when older children and adolescents rebel at efforts to be told familiar biblical narratives because, "I know that story already!" If the objective for teaching Bible content was simply to have people know the factual account of stories, that complaint would often be justified. Unfortunately, focusing on story facts is precisely the way biblical material is often presented by parents and teachers. Instead, if the purpose for teaching biblical content to children is to help them learn more than mere facts, the situation is considerably more complex.

Parents and teachers should have clear objectives in mind before introducing children to Bible narratives. The child needs to begin to learn Bible content in ways that will influence thinking, feeling and actions. It is especially important that Bible material be presented in a simple and clear manner, appropriate to the child's learning level. For when a child misunderstands something the Bible says, there is the risk of developing a negative attitude toward God, as well as to other spiritual concepts. Although it is often possible to correct a faulty piece of information by giving a better answer, attitudes are much more difficult to change. Thus, negative feelings often continue long after the erroneous knowledge that originally created that feeling has been corrected. Fortunately, most children feel positively about God, although their levels of understanding may indeed be immature. This positive feeling can be given a more solid base, however, by appropriately using biblical material.

The influence of Bible stories on children's behavior also raises some important questions. Investigations have repeatedly shown little or no connection between a child's knowledge of the Bible and the way he or she feels or acts. These findings can be explained by understanding the child's great difficulty in making the transfer of learning from one situation to another. Simple knowledge of the facts of a story is not enough to have a significant level of influence on the child to affect personal behavior. Getting the child to say what kind of behavior should be followed is no guarantee that the child will follow that advice.[5]

This problem is by no means limited to early childhood. It has always been the dilemma of moral educators to get people to actually do what they know they should do. Christianity has presented only one effective answer—a spiritual rebirth through acceptance of Jesus Christ as Savior and Lord (see chapter 6). But until the child is capable of a mature commitment, parents and teachers can take specific steps to prepare the child for a personal decision. The same steps are equally appropriate for older children who need to grow in applying their faith. These steps involve helping the child to discover the joy of living in accord with biblical principles.

Activities for Learning About the Bible

Few things communicate the significance of God's Word more effectively to a young child than the attitudes and actions of adults. For example, when a child sees parents reading the Bible, when the child hears them talking about relating God's Word to their everyday experiences, and when the child observes them affirming their dependence upon the Bible as their chief source of inspiration, then the child, too, will be learning to value God's Word. Adults who show by the healthy vigor of their way of living that practicing biblical teachings is a way to show love for the Lord will provide children with attractive models worth emulating. God's Word demonstrated is more convincing than God's Word explained!

The Bible Story
Adults need to carefully consider which sections of the Bible to use with young children. Because the Bible is a book written for adults, by adults and overwhelming about adults, a great deal of its content is difficult for a child. Much of the Old Testament prophecies and the New Testament

Epistles are both uninteresting and unintelligible to little ones.

In selecting those parts of Scripture that will be meaningful to children, parents and teachers should look for stories and verses that contain elements familiar to the child. When the actions of story characters are similar to situations the child has encountered, the child can connect the examples with his or her own behavior.

A key aspect in the effectiveness of any story is the degree to which the child can identify with a person in the narrative.[6]

- The stories of young Samuel assisting in the Tabernacle (see 1 Sam. 2:18-21; 3) or of David being chosen to be king (see 1 Sam. 16) give models of young people who accepted and carried out responsibility successfully. Samuel's situation deserves a word of caution, however. The account of his mother dedicating him to God and taking him to live with the priests can arouse strong negative feelings in some children who fear being abandoned.

- Old Testament stories about the construction, care or repair of the Tabernacle or Temple (see 1 Kings 5—6; 2 Kings 12; 22—23) can be useful in helping a child feel responsibility for the church building. Stress the specific things people did to show their respect for the place of worship. Minimize the unique aspects of sacrificial observances.

- Children respond positively to the stories of Jesus' birth and boyhood (see Matt. 1:18—2:23; Luke 2). They quickly identify with baby Jesus, for here is a person close to their own life experiences. The care of Mary and Joseph for the baby touches responsive chords in children. And the idea of Mary and Joseph frantically looking for 12-year-old Jesus is highly intriguing to every child.

- The story about Jesus and the children (see Matt. 19:13-15) has always been a favorite. Each child can imagine Jesus smiling directly at him or her. This story is effective in helping children develop warm feelings toward Jesus, especially when they sense He is on their side, and not with those stuffy, unfriendly disciples and other adults.

- Zacchaeus (see Luke 19:1-10) is an appealing character to young children, despite his unsavory reputation. They admire his ingenuity to climb a tree in an effort to see over the big people, certainly a familiar problem to little ones. Jesus' recognition of Zacchaeus and His willingness to forgive his wrongdoing adds to the interest in this narrative. For each child has his own memories of unacceptable actions. The assurance of forgiveness at this story's conclusion helps children feel positively about Jesus' consideration for Zacchaeus.

- Jesus' triumphant entry into Jerusalem (see Matt. 21:1-17) can be used to help children express their feelings of love to Jesus. Conclude this account from Bible times by suggesting children sing glad songs to Him to show their love.
- The New Testament accounts of ways Christians helped one another (see Acts 2:42-47; 4:32-37; 6:1-7; 9:36-42) carry a clear message children can understand.

Telling the Bible Story During Activities

A Bible story with which the child can easily identify also aids in transferring truth into real-life experiences. Making this transfer verbally, however, has not proved entirely successful. The child may be able to talk about the point of the story without putting it into effect. A more successful approach is to refer to the story while the child is involved in a real-life situation.

Sunday School teachers can help to accomplish this application of learning through activities in the various learning centers. For example, several children may be playing with blocks, building a rocket ship. The teacher can use conversation about the rocket for a brief account of the creation story from Genesis. A concluding remark, such as "Imagine how great God must be to have created the earth, the moon and the stars just like the Bible says!" is effective in connecting Bible content with the immediate physical activity of the children.

When Allie gave Sharon a turn to rock the doll at the home living area, the teacher nearby commented, "Allie, you are a kind friend to let Sharon rock the doll for a while. I know a story about a young man who made someone very happy, just like you did. Would you like to hear that story?" How could Allie resist? The teacher proceeded to tell both girls about Paul, who wrote to his young friend Timothy, asking him to bring his books and his coat to him. The girls who had just experienced what it means to help someone joined in animated conversation of how Paul must have felt when Timothy arrived. They were also interested in how Timothy felt when he saw how pleased his friend Paul was to see him. The close relationship between the Bible story and the children's actual experience made this an effective learning opportunity.

Teachers often have to arrange such circumstances to provide real-life experiences within the classroom. The parent, however, has the distinct advantage of living with the child in a host of everyday situations. When parents are alert to opportunities to relate Bible stories and truths to the things the child really does, the story can be a good means of instruction. "What you did reminds me of a story in the Bible..." is an effective use of a Bible story as positive reinforcement for desirable behavior.

Visuals

Presenting a Bible story is enhanced by using visual aids. Pictures of the characters in the story help a child visualize them and think of them as real people. A Bible containing attractive Bible story pictures can stimulate a child's interest because any children's book depends to a great extent on its illustrations. Use a picture of a present-day situation that corresponds with a child's personal experience to provide a basis for conversation connecting the Bible story action with the child's experience.

After a teacher told the story of the good Samaritan, she showed the children a picture of a little girl who had fallen off her tricycle and scraped her knee. The picture also showed an older boy who had evidently been playing nearby coming to her side. The teacher asked the children to describe what was happening in the picture. They vividly and accurately told what they saw occurring.

The teacher then asked them to tell what they thought had happened before the accident. These comments became less descriptive and more a projection of their own feelings and experiences.

The teacher then asked what they thought would happen next. By this time, most of the children had firmly identified themselves with one of the two characters in the picture. One boy stated, much to everyone's consternation, that the boy in the picture was now going to take the little girl's tricycle away from her and ride it himself!

"Would that be better than helping the little girl go inside and get her knee fixed?" asked the teacher, hoping the boy would see the error of his judgment.

"Yes," the boy declared, "'cause then he could ride and have a lot of fun."

The teacher tried again. "How do you think he would feel?" she asked.

"He would feel real good, 'cause he was..., no, he'd feel kinda bad 'cause the little girl was still hurt."

"What do you think would make him feel the best?" the teacher asked, relieved that the boy had now seen beyond his interest in that tricycle.

"If he helped her get her knee fixed," the boy affirmed, having successfully wrestled with the same issues Jesus raised in the story He had told.

Drama

Simple dramatic portrayal of Bible-story action also helps a child connect a story to his or her own world. Story play, puppets, filmstrips or videos can make the incident much more real.

A teacher was guiding a group of five-year-olds in acting out the story of the men who cut a hole in the roof to lower a sick man down to Jesus. The teacher gave effective guidance to their efforts. She asked questions such as "How do you think the men felt while they were doing this?" Simple props and a great deal of imagination made the scene live for a few brief moments, although the dialogue was inadequate according to adult standards. At the conclusion, the "sick man" got off his mat and looked "Jesus" in the eye. After saying "Thanks," he looked at the four who had carried him and announced, "Those guys are my friends." That young child obviously got the full effect of the story!

"Tell it again!" are familiar words to those who work with young children. By all means, tell it again. Enhance the story by telling (or reading) it with enthusiasm, which is no easy order on the thirty-fifth retelling. Just watch the reaction of the child to the story's progress. A child is thoroughly delighted with a good retelling of the story when it is possible to identify with the characters and their actions, and when the sequence of events is known.

Occasionally, a sophisticated five- or six-year-old will lean back and declare, "I already know that story." This statement is rarely intended to mean, "So I'm not interested in hearing it again." Usually, the child is simply seeking recognition for his or her "vast" accumulation of knowledge. If the adult affirms the child for knowing the story, and declares enthusiastically, "I hope you like the story; it's one of my favorites!" the child is almost guaranteed to be ready for another retelling.

Although adults tend to stay with a story to find out how it ends, young children enjoy a story most when they already know the ending. Adults moan when someone "gives away the ending," but young children get their enjoyment from anticipating the familiar. Sadly, too many adults impose their perspectives on telling Bible stories, never allowing a child to hear a story often enough for it to become a "favorite." Rather than reserving the Bible story for a specific time in the session, teachers should be looking for every opportunity to tell all or part of the day's story along with every activity children do. By the time the "official" story time comes around, children should have heard the story enough to whet their appetites to say, "Tell it again."

When story time is announced to young children, and if they show signs of reluctance, it is likely their previous story experiences have been less than exciting. The most common mistake in telling a story to young children is to let the story go on too long. A good rule of thumb for how long to make a Bible story is to keep it within one minute of length for every year of the child's age. Thus, a two-year-old child should thoroughly enjoy a two-minute story. A five-year-old is usually ready for a five-minute story. Although some storytellers may be able to keep children's interest longer than that, and some children are able to pay attention longer than that, it is wise to err on the side of getting to the end of the story before the children get to the end of their listening.

Expression

A vital ingredient in storytelling is the adult's enthusiasm! Express feelings of the story in your voice and actions. For instance, look angry or frightened. Yawn to express time for sleep. Smile a big smile to show happiness. Young children quickly sense and reflect these familiar feelings.

To recapture interest that may be waning, switch to a whisper—the most dramatic sound of which the human voice is capable. Then switch back to normal speech to avoid overdoing a good thing.

Questions

Questions, both about the story and about related experiences of the child, also add a rich dimension, making each telling of a story more meaningful. With younger children, ask questions before and after the story, helping children recall the facts of the story. Older children can retain the flow of the narrative long enough to respond to a few relevant questions in the middle of the story action. In either case, if a child flounders while attempting an answer, give additional clues so he or she can answer correctly.

Kindergartners and older children enjoy questions that require reasoning. "Why did Jesus help the sick boy get well again?" Keep these questions simple. Give assistance by helping the child put ideas into words. Children enjoy answering questions that reflect their reactions to the story. "What part of the story did you like best?" "Which person in the story would you like to have for a friend?" Because this requires no single correct answer, each child feels "safe" to offer his or her feelings.

Also ask questions that help the child connect the story action to his or her own experiences. "When have you ever felt sad like Peter did in our story?"

Bible Memorization

Many children are remarkably adept at repeating what they hear. Reciting Bible verses learned by rote, however, has little significance for a child if the words do not convey a clear meaning. To help a child know the meaning of Bible words, relate them to a real situation. For instance, when a child hears Galatians 6:10 ("Let us do good to all people"), spoken at a time when he or she is being kind to someone, the child will relate those words to his or her actions: "David, when you helped Lisa pick up the puzzle pieces she dropped, you were doing just what the Bible says. The Bible says, 'Let us do good to all people.'" Commending a child for acts of kindness makes the desired behavior attractive.

Showing the child pictures of people doing good, as you help the child recall times when good actions were experienced, adds to understanding the concept of doing good. Commending a child for acts of goodness also helps make the desired behavior attractive. Again and again with conversation, songs, explanations and pictures, build for the child a groundwork of familiarity with understanding. Memorization may occur along with these experiences, but it is not the aim.

Beginning to Use the Bible

Even before children learn to read, they can be given pleasurable hands-on experiences with the Book itself. Then, as children begin to read, they can also begin to use the Bible for themselves. Basic Bible skills can be taught to any child who is at least beginning to learn to read.

Although the Bible is a large, somewhat intimidating book, beginning readers are motivated enough to master this skill so that they will thoroughly enjoy opportunities to "find" some things in the Bible for themselves. Older children who have experienced reading difficulties also benefit from these experiences, as long as they are not pressured or made to feel inadequate.

Look at words with an adult. Instead of simply quoting the Bible, or telling about what it says, take a moment and actually open the Bible to the page where the verse or story is located. Point to the verse or paragraph as you tell the child, "This is where our Bible says...." Some parents and teachers find it helpful to underline or highlight the passage to which they refer. If the child is interested in letters, words and names, point out several key words on the page. "Here is Jesus' name. It starts with a J, just like Jeff's name and Jamie's name. Look just below my finger and see if you can find Jesus' name again. Very good!"

Find familiar words. Once a passage has been located, most beginning readers can locate at least one familiar word or more. Even if the only words the child knows are "a," "an" or "the," the child still feels a sense of accomplishment in being able to recognize them. Hints are perfectly legal if needed to help a child find a more significant word or name: "Look for David's name. David begins with a capital *D*."

Notice the name of the book. While looking at a passage, call attention to the name of the book at the top of the page. Even if the name is too difficult for the child to read, pointing to the name as you read it aloud helps to build familiarity with Bible books, and acquaints the child with where to look on the page for helpful information.

Notice the preceding and following books. Establish a pattern of noting the Bible books that are immediate neighbors to the one being used. This helps a child gain a sense of the sequence of books and in time aids greatly in the ability to move quickly through the Bible's pages.

Locate the book. Most children ages six and up can learn to use the contents page in the front of the Bible to locate a book. This is easiest if the child's Bible has an alphabetical contents page, not just the standard one that lists the books in order.

A shortcut. To quickly find certain Bible books, *first* have the child hold the Bible closed, then try to open it as close to the middle as possible. In most Bibles, this action will put the child in or very near the book of Psalms or Proverbs. (A Bible that has a concordance at the end can throw this search off a little.) Because many Bible verses used with children are found in Psalms or Proverbs, this technique is very useful. *Next*, have the child hold the front half of the Bible and divide it in half. In most Bibles, the child will open to 1 Samuel or very close to it. A few pages back brings the child to stories of the judges (Deborah, Gideon, Samson and so on) and Ruth. And immediately at hand are the stories of Samuel, Saul and David, followed by the narratives of the kings and prophets. *Finally*, have the child divide the second half of the Bible in half. In most Bibles, the child will open to Matthew, and be well on the way to locating stories from the life of Jesus.

Locate the verse. It only takes a moment to point out to a child how Bible books are divided into chapters and verses to make it easy to quickly find a verse or story. Point out the chapter divisions, as well as the chapter numbers, at the top of the pages. Within a chapter, challenge the child to find the smaller numbers that mark the beginning of the verses.

Find the answer. As reading skills improve, children quickly become capable of reading most words in most Bible verses. (Biblical names and occasional big words may cause them to stumble.) Beginning readers, however, often have to focus so much energy just on "reading" words, that also trying to understand what the words mean rarely occurs to them. Even more advanced readers do not automatically use reading as a means to gain information, especially when reading something a teacher or parent has assigned.

To nudge a child into looking for meaning in what he or she reads, ask a question, then let the child find the answer in the verse being read. The child's initial response will be to simply read the verse, then look up with an expression that says, *I guess the answer's in there somewhere. You figure it out.* A further nudge is often needed to get the child to look at the verse again, this time looking for the word or words that tell the answer to the question.

Rephrase the verse. One of the best ways to check on a child's understanding of a verse or statement is to ask him or her to say the same thing by using other words. Good ways to phrase this assignment include, "How could you tell a younger child what this verse means?" or "How would you explain what this story is about to a friend who had never heard it before?"

Apply the point. Whether the child is a nonreader, a beginning reader or an advanced reader, always take time to consider how Bible content applies to life today. It is never enough to learn what it says, or even what it means. We must consistently encourage children to explore what we should do about it now. Questions are effective ways to stimulate thinking about the implications of what has been heard or read:

- "Why do you think this verse/story is important for us to know?"
- "What could we do that would show we have learned to live as this verse/story teaches?"
- "Who do you know who is a good example of what this verse/story teaches?"

The Child and Prayer

"Dear God, thank You for my mother and daddy and for Carol and Don and for Tippy. Help me be a good helper when we mow the lawn tomorrow."

Billy's prayer demonstrated a young child's amazing sense of the reality of God. He expressed concern for the important people in his life by listing them in his prayer. Sometimes he may offer a catalog of all the good things he wants for himself. He enjoys prayer, for it gives him a sense of security and of mastery. The security comes from a sense that God hears him and will make sure that all goes well. Mastery is the feeling that comes from being able to talk directly to someone important, knowing He will do what is best.

The child, however, has little awareness of what prayer really is.[7] Jeffrey, age four, talked of his prayers as literal things: "And then the wind comes and blows them up to heaven where God is." Anna, age five, believed that failure to get the expected answer was because of faulty transmission on her part. "You have to know the right words to make them (prayers) work."

One little girl stopped saying her bedtime prayers after her family moved to a new house. It finally dawned on her parents that when they had lived just a few blocks from the church building, Melanie had no difficulty in believing God actually heard her prayers. But when they moved across town, it strained her childish faith to believe her prayers could still be heard all the way back at "God's house."

These are common kinds of statements children make about prayer, and they illustrate the twin dilemma caused by the child's vague notions of what prayer is, coupled with a strong certainty that this notion, whatever it may be, is correct. The child's ideas about prayer are highly colored by ideas of God, depending to a great extent on what the child believes God to be like. If God is a physical being, and either lives somewhere in that church building or high atop a huge cloud, getting a message to Him by praying can seem to be a major challenge.

Even when the child accepts the idea that God listens to our prayers, a child's prayers also reflect other dimensions of child-level thought. It is no surprise that the great proportion of prayers by children are self-centered, fitting perfectly the basic outlook of the egocentric child. When a child prays for another, requests are often phrased in terms of that person's relationship to the child. For example, five-year-old Dina prayed, "And please help Mommy and Daddy to love me." Because a loving relationship is the most pleasant way of life for Dina, the prayer is very natural. She is not yet fully aware of her parents as people who have a life separate from her, who sometimes do things that have no relationship to her. That shocking revelation will come after a few more years of family living.

Similarly, children are much more interested in their own prayers than in what anyone else prays. Because much of the adult prayer observed by children, especially at church, is rather lengthy, (very lengthy, according to children), and therefore, rather boring (very boring, according to children), other people's prayers tend to be of only limited interest to a child.

In general, children under the age of seven usually explain prayer in terms of asking God for things. They tend to assume it is God's obligation to do what they ask, and it is not uncommon for a young child to get angry with God if a prayer is not answered. From seven to nine years of age, it is typical for children to begin to explain prayer as talking with God, not just asking for things. Asking, however, is still big on the child's agenda, although much of it is now directed on behalf of others, including their pets. Instead of being angry with God if a prayer is not answered, the child at this age tends to question whether or not the prayer was phrased properly or was sincere enough.[8]

Perhaps because the child's conceptions of prayer are so vague, much of the child's feelings, thoughts and practice concerning prayer will be determined by the adult models the child observes. If their models' prayers are long, formal dissertations to God, the child is likely to conclude that prayer is dull. If the prayers of adults are kept brief, informal and deal with matters of concern to the child, prayer will be seen as positive.

Activities for Learning About Prayer

Adult models. A child needs repeated opportunities to hear adults pray. The adult's attitude of reverence and sincerity is keenly felt by a child. Although the child may not understand all the words, he or she senses that talking to God is a very real experience. A child who consistently hears expressions of thanksgiving and praise to God for His loving care, His gifts and His forgiveness soon recognizes that God is loving and cares about people.

When teachers or parents express their own feelings in prayer, the child sees appropriate models for expressing his or her own responses. Prayer is then not merely a formula, it is an expression of real feelings.

For example, Richie's family vacation was unexpectedly cut short by an urgent business crisis. Richie heard his dad pray, "Lord, You know how disappointed we are about having to go home now. We are really unhappy. Please help us to remember the good times we had this week and to be glad for them." The drive home was spent reminiscing about the enjoyments of their week, rather than sulking about the days that were missed.

Bedtime. Many parents find that bedtime is a much more pleasant time of day for all concerned when it is used to recall the happy things of the day. Following a relaxed conversation about the favorite experiences of both child and parent, Mom or Dad may simply say, "Dear God, I'm thankful for the good time we had at dinner tonight. We enjoyed the food, and being together was fun. Thank You for my wonderful family." Then ask the child for what he or she would like to thank God.

Bedtime can also be an effective time to clear the air of unpleasant feelings caused by family conflicts. Take care in these situations to avoid using prayers to preach to the child. Praying that God will help Billy not to be such a stinker tomorrow can only serve to build resistance in the child.

One mother wisely prayed after a particularly trying evening, "Father, I am sorry I got so upset with Brian today. Help me to be more patient." Nothing was said that Brian should also pray similarly. But several months later, after hearing similar kinds of confessions and requests for help from his parents, he closed his prayer with the postscript: "And Jesus, I think I was too fussy today. Help me to be nicer tomorrow."

Memorized prayers. Parents and teachers sometimes teach a young child an easily memorized prayer poem as the first way to talk to God. Most children enjoy using memorized prayers at times. The rhyme and rhythm appeal to children. Recitation also provides the satisfaction of praying just like someone else, which can be very reassuring at times. The memorized prayer, however, tends to be rattled off with little thought to meaning. Also, these kinds of prayers are sometimes used to cover adult embarrassment about not feeling at ease with spontaneous prayers. In any case, just as parents buy larger clothes as their child grows, so they also need to provide the opportunity to move beyond the rote prayers of younger years.

Repeating prayers. Sometimes it is helpful to have a child repeat a prayer, phrase by phrase. This experience can be a first step toward the child's using his or her own words. Or, it can be drudgery, convincing the child that prayer must be a complicated process that is obviously too difficult for a child to do without help.

Guidelines. When praying with a child, bring your prayer to the child's level, rather than expecting the child to pray at your level. This does not mean "dumbing down" your prayer. Rather, it means praying so that the child is not just an observer, waiting until the grown-up is done so that he or she can have a turn. Instead, think of the child as joining with you in prayer, using your prayer as an example.

- Keep your prayer short. Even Jesus, when teaching His adult disciples to pray, gave them an example of just three sentences (see Matt. 6:9-13).
- Keep your sentences short. Short sentences are easy for children to follow (and imitate), and they help you focus on keeping things simple.

- Avoid symbolism or flowery expressions! Children do not comprehend these figures of speech. For prayer to be meaningful, a child should understand what he or she is saying.
- Talk to the Lord about things within the child's experience.
- Speak naturally. Avoid using archaic terms, such as "thy," "thou" and "thee."

As a child's language skills increase, it becomes easier to express feelings in his or her own words. The child often needs some guidance, however, to focus on what to say. A vague, "Thank You, God, for all my blessings," encompasses more than a young child's mind can grasp! To center the child's thinking, ask simple questions to help the child recognize a specific way God shows His care.

"Karen, what did you eat for breakfast this morning?" "Andrew, who cooked your cereal? (combed your hair? polished your shoes? brought you home from church?)" "Jon, what other ways do your mother and daddy help you?" "Joey, God planned for you to have a family! If you would like to say 'Thank You, God, for my family,' you may come and stand beside me while we pray."

Then, lead the prayer. "Dear God, we thank You for the families of boys and girls here today. We are glad You love each one of us. In Jesus' name, Amen." This kind of participation may help a child who is reticent about praying aloud feel as though he or she is a part of your prayer.

Of course, teachers must be alert to any child in the group whose family is composed of people other than the traditional members. Children living with a single parent, foster parents, grandparents, aunts and so on need to be assured that their families are accepted. "Mrs. Davis is your family. God planned for her to take care of you."

Spontaneous prayer. Express your own feelings in prayer while in the middle of activities with the child. This gives an appropriate model for expressing personal responses to God. It also shows that we can talk to God at any time. Prayer is then not merely a formula—it is an expression of real feelings.

To respond in heartfelt thanks to God, a child should be aware of specific ways God provides for needs. This awareness of God's loving care is often the first step toward expressing feelings of gratitude. In your daily or classroom routine, call your child's attention to items that he or she can see, smell, taste, touch and hear. Then relate the experience to God's care. For instance, as you pour a cup of juice, say, "God made oranges so you can drink this good-tasting juice. Isn't God good to you! Let's thank God for this juice."

During a child's activities, you'll discover opportunities to guide the child in brief prayers. During these informal moments when a child is fully absorbed in an interesting project, you may find it helpful to suggest simple prayers about whatever interests the child has. For instance, as a child arranges a bouquet of flowers, ask simple questions about the flowers' colors, fragrances and unique shapes. When you sense the child's feelings of wonder and awe, which is often a reflection of your own, quietly say, "Sharon, we can thank God for making these flowers for us." If the child seems unsure of what to say, you can suggest, "You can say, 'Thank You, God, for these flowers.'"

As a child busily works (cutting, drawing, painting), say, "Janet, just look at the interesting work your hands can do! God made your hands with fingers so you can hold scissors. For what other things do you need your fingers? Let's thank God right now for your fingers. You can say, 'Thank You, God, for my fingers.'"

When a child prays in his or her own words, assist if needed to help the child complete the prayer. Simply ask, "Would you like me to help you think of words you want to say to God?" Avoid making a child feel his or her prayer is wrong or poorly expressed.

Prayer for others. To help children know they can help others by praying for them, gather pictures of a missionary, your pastor and/or several teachers your child knows. Talk with the child about ways each of these people helps others learn of the Lord. Use words the child understands. Then ask God to help these people do their jobs well.

The Lord's Prayer. Kindergartners and older children are interested in knowing that the Lord's Prayer is a prayer Jesus taught and that it is recorded in our Bibles. The phrases are long, however, and many of the words are beyond the understanding of a young child. ("Give us this day our jelly bread," one child prayed.) When a child is elementary age, learning and memorizing this significant part of Scripture will be a more meaningful experience than during the years of early childhood. If children are in situations where they hear this prayer, it is helpful to give simple explanations for some of the phrases. "Jesus taught us to call God our Father because God is like a perfect father or mother who always loves and helps us."

Group prayer. In group settings, avoid putting children on the spot for prayer "performances." Praying in front of others may cause a child to focus attention on the group, and not on God. A child's prayer is likely to be more natural and sincere when offered privately or in a small-group activity, rather than in a larger group where the child is likely to be more self-conscious.

When we spend time each day talking with God, when we turn first to Him in an anxious moment, and when our thinking and our plans reflect our dependence upon His guidance, then children will likely sense through our attitudes and actions the reality of prayer in our own lives. Our task is to earnestly share with children our deep beliefs in prayer. The result of our work is then in the hands of the Holy Spirit.

Notes

1. M. B. Evans, "Religious Ideas and Attitudes of the Young Child" (Ph.D. diss., Wayne State University, 1964).

2. H. Munsinger, *Fundamentals of Child Development* (New York: Holt, Rinehart and Winston, 1971), p. 124.

3. Ronald Goldman, *Religious Thinking from Childhood to Adolescence* (New York: Seabury Press, 1964), p. 21.

4. J. G. Kenwrick, *The Religious Quest* (London: S.P.C.K., 1955), p. 23.

5. Munsinger, *Fundamentals of Child Development*, p. 205.

6. Eleanor Zimmerman, *Doctrine for 3's to 5's* (Philadelphia: Lutheran Church Press, 1963), p. 49.

7. D. Long, D. Elkind, and B. Spilka, "The Child's Conception of Prayer," *Journal for the Scientific Study of Religion* 6 (1967): 102-108.

8. David Elkind, *Understanding Your Child from Birth to Sixteen* (Boston: Allyn and Bacon, 1994), p. 152.

CHAPTER

6

The Child and Jesus

"Why did Jesus live on earth?"
"God wanted people to know He loved them and some couldn't hear His inside whisper, so He sent Jesus to tell them out loud."[1]

This answer by a five-year-old boy is very perceptive. It recognizes the basic purpose of the Incarnation and the existence of a special relationship between Jesus and God the Father. This doctrine has mystified theologians for nearly two thousand years, let alone five-year-olds.

Who was the man, Jesus Christ? What was the nature of His relationship with the Father? How was He similar to and different from any other human being? Where is He now, and what is His present role? These questions, studied by scholars, preachers and laymen since the time of Christ, are at the very core of Christianity. They are also similar to the kinds of questions a young child asks about Jesus: Is God Jesus' daddy? Was Jesus a little baby or a big man? Where is Jesus now? The answers children give to their own questions are not always as mature as the one given at the beginning of this chapter. Children's responses do, however, often show the beginnings of insight into the nature of Jesus.

Jesus and God

The most frequent problem investigators, teachers and parents have found in the child's thinking about Jesus is the overwhelming tendency to confuse Jesus and God.[2] Most children under the age of six will use the two names interchangeably. Ask a child, "Who made the world?" and you are as likely to be told that Jesus is the Creator as you are to hear that God made everything. Show a picture of Jesus and ask a child who it is. Either reply can be expected.

An adult's attempt to clarify the child's view often serves only to increase the difficulty. Efforts to emphasize the distinctions between Jesus and God run the risk of creating two Gods in the child's mind. Because the overlapping of Jesus and God has a sold backing in biblical teaching, it should not be viewed as a total error, but rather as an incomplete, childish understanding.

Attractiveness of Jesus

An important aspect of the young child's thinking about Jesus is the strong attraction most youngsters exhibit toward Him. Generally, children who have had any exposure to stories about Jesus believe He is warm, sympathetic and pleasant. Rarely does a child express feelings of antagonism or fear toward Jesus, in contrast to occasional outbursts that a child may direct against God, teachers, parents or other authority figures.

The reason for these almost unanimous good feelings seems to be that the stories and songs the child hears about Jesus are almost exclusively of His loving, supportive nature. Judgmental or punishment references are generally portrayed in terms of God, the Father. Also, the child identifies strongly with stories of Jesus as a baby and a child, as well as the concept of Jesus as God's Son. Jesus tends to be viewed as the child's ally against an adult-dominated and sometimes hostile world.

Death and Resurrection

When can a child begin to understand the significance of Jesus' death and resurrection? Investigations into the young child's view of death have found that in modern societies, children under the age of six have vague notions of what death involves. This is to be expected with children who are insulated from death—who have never experienced the loss of anyone who was an important part of their daily lives. Prior to the age of five or six, the child does not realize that death is permanent, viewing it merely as another form of ordinary separation.[3] Children often expect physical resurrections of dead birds, pets and grandparents. Thus, the resurrection of Jesus is seen as very normal, not at all extraordinary. The young child has little difficulty accepting the facts of the Resurrection because the meaning of death is vague. Rather than emphasizing the miraculous nature of Jesus' resurrection with young children, the focus should simply be "Jesus is living, and we are glad!"

Salvation

A sensitive area in the thinking of those who are concerned about a child's Christian education is the question of the child's salvation. Mainstream Christianity has consistently maintained that the focal issue of any person's spiritual life is the question of a personal relationship with Jesus Christ. A commitment to trust in Christ's sacrificial death is proclaimed by the Church as the only means of finding eternal life. Many Christians have thus advocated seeking to lead children into that commitment as early in their lives as possible.

How early in life is it really possible for a person to properly make such a commitment? Some people contend children as young as two years old are ready; others maintain any decision made before adolescence is suspect. Some of this disagreement is based on opposing theological views of the spiritual status of the infant: Is the child born innocent or already tainted by original sin?

Some are concerned about situations they have observed in which children, encouraged to make early commitments to Christ, seemed to have been inoculated with just enough Christianity to make them immune to the real thing when they got older. Most of the attention, however, seems to focus on determining the age at which the child can really be considered to be responsible for his or her actions and decisions. Thus, many believe that the mental and emotional age, rather than the chronological age, of the child is the determining factor.

Responsibility. Some real problems are involved in applying the principle of accountability to children under the age of six. For a child to be considered guilty of sin, and thus in need of cleansing and forgiveness, the child must be able to understand the significance of his or her actions. More is involved than merely recognizing that certain actions are acceptable and others are not. A valid decision demands that the child be capable of accepting responsibility for actions and their consequences.

This is a critical point because in very few areas of life is a child under age 6, even under 12, considered capable of personal responsibility. When is a child allowed to settle the question of whether or not to attend school? When is a child considered mature enough to decide whether or not to brush teeth, do chores or take medicine? Is a visit to the doctor within a child's realm of choice? A child may be allowed to choose the color of shirt to wear, the flavor of ice cream to eat or the games to play with friends. Can it be expected that these experiences give the child enough background in making choices to enable making a decision that extends into eternity?

Vulnerability. The matter is further complicated by how easily a young child can be manipulated. A child is extremely vulnerable to almost any kind of pressure. Most children keenly desire to please the adults in their lives. They endure innumerable inconveniences to earn a smile, a pat or a word of commendation. Recognition from adults is one of the strongest motivators in the child's experience. The admired parent or teacher who asks the child, "Would you like to ask Jesus to forgive your sins?" may be more likely to have the child respond out of a desire to cooperate than from a true conviction or understanding of what is happening. A desire to do what other children are doing is also a powerful factor in leading many children to announce their intention to become Christians.

Changing interests. Children are also notorious for their changeableness. Although many children are adept at displaying their wills, often with fierce stubbornness, the specific issue at any one time is very much a product of that moment. It is not the result of careful planning and evaluation by the child. Every parent and teacher utilizes the effective tactic of changing the child's unacceptable behavior by substituting another attraction to capture interest. What a child considers a matter of life and death one moment is totally forgotten the next. Also, a child's perceptive question may lead an adult to think the youngster is all primed for some significant information. In reality, attention may have quickly followed another path, leaving the helpful adult in mid explanation.

Repentance. Repentance is another issue of importance, for it is frequently mentioned in the Bible as a necessary ingredient of salvation. Although a child may express sorrow for a specific misdeed, it is highly questionable that this regret is more than distress resulting from unpleasant consequences. The child's difficulty with broad concepts makes it difficult to understand forgiveness for sin in general. The idea of repentance as turning away from a whole pattern of selfish behavior requires a sophisticated level of reasoning.

Symbolism. Further complicating the matter is the tendency for adults to explain or illustrate salvation by using symbolic terms such as "born again" or "asking Jesus into your heart." The learned teacher, Nicodemus (see John 3:3-21), was not the last person to misunderstand the meaning of "born again," and countless children have conjured up bizarre interpretations of having Jesus "in my heart." Many children, obviously thinking of the physical organ that pumps blood, become concerned about how Jesus could actually get *into* their hearts, and what effect that might have on the heart's ability to keep beating.

Six-year-old Stephanie was confident in her declaration that Jesus was in her heart. When asked, "How did Jesus come into your heart?" she replied quickly, "I asked Him, and He came in?" When asked again, "But *how* did He come in?" she thought a moment, then an impish smirk appeared on her face. In a high-pitched, rather silly voice, she explained, "He got really teeny-tiny, and slid down my tongue." Stephanie was old enough to realize that her explanation was nonsensical, but she was still too young to think in anything but concrete, physical terms.

Eight-year-old Andrew had a different kind of concern. At bedtime one night, he asked, "When I die, how is Jesus going to get *out* of my heart?" The phrases "becoming God's child" or "a member of God's family" (based on John 1:12) are also symbolic. The imagery of a family relationship, however, tends to create less misunderstanding than the other terms commonly used.

The above analysis is, of course, limited to a human perspective. The process of regeneration is ultimately beyond all human understanding. The exact way the Holy Spirit works to draw a person to God is truly a mystery. Testimonials of many people's childhood experiences give support to very real spiritual encounters at remarkably young ages. The child raised in a supportive, Christian environment may express a desire to accept Jesus. Recognizing that children are prone to act as though they understand what adults are talking about when in reality they do not, however, should cause adults to be sensitive in addressing this vital issue. Sensitive questioning and an openness to the Spirit's guidance can guide parents and teachers to know how to respond. (See "Guiding the Child Toward Jesus" later in this chapter.)

Activities for Learning About Jesus

A basic rule of thumb for helping children begin to know about Jesus is to place the major emphasis on His humanity. If we first introduce Jesus from the perspective of His deity, we make the child's learning task far more complex. Jesus recognized this problem Himself as He taught His disciples and other followers. He called them to follow Him, to observe and learn from Him. Only gradually did they come to see Him as the Son of God. And then, it was the result of a special revelation from God to Peter (see Matt. 16:16,17).

Similarly, it is best to allow the natural attraction to the person of Jesus to draw the child closer to the Master. Having that kind of foundation, evidence of Jesus' divine nature will take on more significance for the child as concepts mature.

Relating Jesus' Life to the Child's Experience

Infancy and boyhood. Jesus' infancy and boyhood are of special interest to children. Although the Bible tells very little of these early years, it does clearly state that young Jesus "grew in wisdom and stature, and in favor with God and men" (Luke 2:52). Children's fascination with the process of growth, especially their own transformation from infancy to childhood, helps them to identify with Jesus. Also, talking about ways Jesus grew helps to alleviate some of the uncertainty about whether He was a baby or a man. Many children have seen Him only in those two stages of life and need to see Him also as a growing boy.

To make Jesus' boyhood meaningful to the child, relate it to some of the child's firsthand experiences. Comment about ways Jesus helped His family. Knowing that Jesus went to school and to the Temple are of real interest when compared to the child's own familiar experiences.

Jesus the carpenter. Another facet of Jesus' life that is of keen interest to children is His work as a carpenter. Most four- and five-year-olds are capable of using small hammers and saws to construct rather amazing structures. Provide them with some soft wood, roofing nails and a place to work. Of course, some preliminary instruction and a bit of understanding guidance are necessary for safety. What better setting could there be, then, for an informal discussion about the kinds of things Jesus might have made in Joseph's carpentry shop. This activity also provides opportunities to talk about the strength and skill required to build with wood. This kind of conversation helps children to see Jesus as a strong and capable man.

Jesus the teacher and example. Children are also interested in knowing that Jesus taught people many things about God. Teachers are important people in the young child's life. The title of "teacher" is helpful to their understanding of Jesus. Help children know specific ways Jesus not only said good things, but also did many good, helpful actions. Also, explain how He avoided acting selfishly. Link Jesus' positive examples to the child's own experiences. For example, "Josh, you were really kind to give Tiffany a turn to ride your tricycle. I think that is just what Jesus would have done." Also, help children to become aware that adults also try to emulate Jesus' example. "I'll be glad to help you fix that truck, Bryan. Jesus always helped people, and I want to be like Him."

If Jesus' example is used in an effort to motivate better efforts from the child, however, it can take on the same nagging tone as, "Why can't you be neat like your sister?" This is highly damaging to a child's self-concept! The child builds resentments toward what appear to be unattainable expectations. Thus, it is wise to avoid statements such as "Jesus wouldn't like that" or "Don't you want to be like Jesus?" This approach is likely to earn the response one mother got when she asked her three-year-old to help pick up her toys "because we love Jesus." The little girl thought for a moment, then said, "You love Jesus, Mommy. You pick up the toys."

Jesus and miracles. Talking about Jesus' actions leads naturally into considering His miracles. The child has little difficulty accepting the reality of the miracles, but has trouble applying that information to personal experience. Guide the conversation so the child understands Jesus did wonderful things to help people because He loved these people. For the child, the importance of these miraculous deeds is not so much the deeds themselves, but the purpose they served. "Jesus loved those men so much that He did not want them to be sick. He made them well because He loved them."

Should a child ask, "But how did He do that?" giving a simple answer is best. "Jesus is God. I don't know *how* Jesus made the dead man live again, but I do know that Jesus always used His power to show His great love." None of the child's faith is damaged by hearing an adult say, "This is one of the things about Jesus and God that I don't fully understand. God is so great, there are things about Him no one can explain. But we can know for sure that Jesus loves us." Always bring the focus back to what we *can* know for sure, rather than dwelling on that which is unexplainable.

Pictures of Jesus. Seeing pictures of Jesus helps the child feel a closer relationship to Him. Sooner or later, a child is bound to ask if Jesus really looked like the person in the painting. This question usually arises after a child has seen several pictures by various artists. Simply explain that the picture is merely what one artist thought Jesus may have looked like because no one drew His picture when He was on earth.

Songs about Jesus. Many of a child's ideas about Jesus are formed from singing songs about Him. Songs about Jesus are effective in influencing children's concepts and feelings because words set to a melody are often repeated and tend to become authoritative definitions.

- "Jesus Loves Me" has had a powerful influence on children's awareness of Jesus' love for them. (However, the words of the stanzas are generally not understood by children under the age of six, largely because the word order is often switched to achieve rhyming (i.e., "this I know" instead of "I know this").

- "Jesus Loves the Little Children" has also communicated the idea that Jesus loves children, although its interracial message gets blurred in the line "Red and yellow, black and white." This list generally comes across to a child as just miscellaneous colors people like. Efforts to identify these colors with people's skin tones often meet firm resistance from children who are rightly convinced, "Nobody has red skin!" The idea of people having yellow and white skin gets the same reaction, even in groups populated with both Asian and Caucasian children. The literal viewpoint of the child often allows only black to stand as a genuine skin color.

These examples provide a warning signal to adults to look at songs from a child's perspective. Decide if the message that comes across is the one intended. One teacher discovered, after trying to teach her five-year-olds to sing "Fairest Lord Jesus," that her children interpreted the first line to be a reference that Jesus did not cheat. The children's ideas certainly did not fit with the song's intent to compare Jesus as greater than all the wonders of creation.

Relating Christmas and Easter to the Child's Experience

The two most significant times in the Christian year, Christmas and Easter, center around pivotal events in the life of Jesus. These Christian festivals have special attraction for children. Christmas and Easter pose real problems in teaching, however, both because of the great confusion between the religious and secular aspects of the occasions, as well as the challenge of communicating the significance of the original events in a way children can understand.

Four-year-old Luis thought he had Easter analyzed when he explained that "it was when Jesus arose from the grave and the Easter bunny hopped out after Him."

CHRISTMAS. It is pointless to engage in further hand-wringing about the way Christmas has become the most materialistic time of the year as we celebrate the birth of the man who said, "Do not store up for yourselves treasures on earth,....But seek first his kingdom and his righteousness" (Matt. 6:19,33).

Sadly, most Christian families spend far more time and energy on the secular aspects of Christmas than on the spiritual, all the while muttering at how "society" has corrupted Christmas. Without diminishing the pleasure of Christmas as a family time and the joy of giving and receiving gifts (although the massive quantities of frivolous presents do tend to make a mockery of the spirit of Christmas), thoughtful steps can be taken to increase the spiritual significance of Christmas for children.

In seeking to make the spiritual meaning of Christmas and Easter important to children, the attitude of the adults is the key. If the importance of Jesus' birth and resurrection is not truly meaningful to parents or teachers, attempts to force children to respond to pious pronouncements will be self-defeating. The child will take his or her cue primarily from those things that are of greatest interest to adults. The instructions God gave to Jewish families for celebrating their deliverance from Egypt provide a good model for Christian family celebrations. The combination of good food, expressions of joy, and brief, simple explanations of the meaning of the event is a powerful way to help children both enjoy and begin to understand why these celebrations are really important.

The manger scene. The crèche has long been used as a focus of interest during the Christmas season. Allow children to participate in assembling the manger scene. Give them an opportunity to move the figures as the story is told. Many children frequently return to the crèche during the holidays to play with the figures, retelling the story as they do.

Decorations. Many Christmas decorations originated as symbols of Christian truth. It is a beautiful thing for a child to be introduced to the tree, the holly wreath and the colored lights as things other than just colorful backdrops for mountains of presents. A book of Christmas customs can be an enriching addition to any home or classroom—for adults as well as for children.

Picture books. One or more colorful picture books of the Christmas story should be used throughout the holidays. Bedtime for a week or so before Christmas can be built around reading parts of the story.

Television and video. Television—which bombards the home with Santa Claus, nebulous exaltation of something called the Christmas Spirit, and never-ending sales pitches for gift ideas—also provides occasional opportunities for viewing dramatic portrayals of the Christmas story. Selective viewing (or video renting), which should be a pattern in any home, can make television an asset rather than the liability it frequently is.

A birthday party. Emphasizing the birthday aspect of Christmas strikes a responsive note in children. A birthday party for Jesus may be a little difficult for children to appreciate when they cannot see the guest of honor. However, they certainly enjoy talking about what Mary and Joseph might have done for Jesus on His second or fifth birthday. Talk with children about their own birthdays to help them relate the growth of Jesus to their own experiences.

Carol singing. When families and church groups enjoy a time of carol singing, they should include "Away in a Manger" or a song or two that the younger members are learning at church. Starting off with "Jingle Bells" (which young children enjoy at the oddest times of year) also gets children involved. (Note: Including another children's favorite, "Rudolph, the Red-Nosed Reindeer," can introduce a brief statement about the imaginary parts of celebrating Christmas before the true story of Jesus' birth is discussed.) A fun thing for a family is to spend an evening writing some new carols. Using tunes familiar to the child, write new words to tell the Christmas story.

Giving gifts. Another meaningful family or class experience is to give gifts to others outside the group. Several weeks before Christmas, meet with children to decide whom to surprise and what to give. Often the gift can be something the whole group can participate in making, such as baking cookies or making pages for a picture book. If everyone cannot share in making the gift, decorating the wrapping paper can be a joint project. Gadget printing (dipping any common object or sliced fruit or vegetable onto a sponge soaked with tempera paint, then pressing it onto paper to create a design) is a simple yet creative and colorful way in which even the youngest can participate. Then, as the presents are delivered, they all can truly feel they have had a part in the project.

Some families vary their giving projects from year to year—they plan something special for neighbors, a nearby rest home, an orphanage or perhaps the children's Sunday School teachers. By including the children in planning the project, as well as working on it, the children can have a meaningful experience of giving without seeking to receive in return.

EASTER. What can the Easter story mean to the young child who possesses a vague concept of death? In the weeks preceding Easter, give the child some experiences by using examples that deal with life and death. This can be done most simply with the life cycle of plants. Let your child observe seeds growing to maturity as well as seeing the death of a leaf or cut flower. Conversation about the death of a pet or a wild animal will be helpful, leading the child toward understanding the physical finality of death. As in any other area of life, the child will absorb the attitude of the adult. Parents who are fearful of death and become nervous when it is discussed will arouse the same feelings in the child. If parents can talk about death calmly, and answer questions honestly, the child will accept it as a natural process.

Conversations about separation help the child to understand, rather than fear, the sorrow that usually surrounds death. All children have experienced the pangs of temporary separation from parents, thus they can begin to understand why people are often sad when a person dies. In talking about the reaction of Jesus' friends when He was crucified, one teacher explained, "Jesus' friends were very sad when Jesus died because they thought they would never see Him again. Some of them even cried, for they loved Him very much. Can you imagine how very happy they were when they found out that Jesus wasn't dead anymore! They must have laughed and hugged each other and told all their friends, 'Jesus isn't dead. He is alive! Jesus is living!'"

During Easter, emphasize the joy we feel because Jesus is living. Although the simple facts of the Crucifixion story can be told, avoid the gruesome aspects. A young child is often overwhelmed emotionally at these details.

Pictures. Suggest that a child paint or color a picture after hearing the story of Jesus' resurrection. This art experience provides a way of seeing what was most important in the story from the child's perspective. After the drawing or painting is completed, talk with the child about this art. If the child has any negative, fearful feelings about the story or about death, these will probably come to light in the conversation about the painting.

Questions. After hearing the Resurrection story, a child may ask, "Where is Jesus now?"

- "Jesus is with us" is a helpful answer. If the child then questions how that can be, explain, "Jesus is God's Son. He promised to always be with those who love Him."
- "Jesus is in heaven" is another answer easily accepted by the questioning child. The reaction to this information, however, depends on the child's concept of heaven and of God. If the child understands heaven as a happy place where God and Jesus live, and where no one is sick or hurt, the feelings will likely be positive.

If the child is confused by how Jesus can be both in heaven and with us at the same time, or how He can be with many people in a variety of places, say, "I don't know how Jesus can do that, either. Because He is God's Son, He can do things we don't understand. That shows how great He really is."

Guiding the Child Toward Jesus

To help, rather than hinder, a child move toward God, ask questions that will show the degree of understanding the child has about salvation, including his or her level of commitment to that belief. Avoid asking leading questions that put words in the child's mouth or that can be answered by saying yes or no.

Five-year-old Jason's father was pleased when his son announced, "Daddy, I want Jesus to come into my heart."

Dad responded by saying, "I'm glad you're thinking about this, Jason, because it's the most important decision you will ever make. Tell me, what do you like most about Jesus?"

This question was less threatening than a straight "Why do you want to become a Christian?" and thus was easier for Jason to answer. Also, his father hoped it would reveal some of Jason's thoughts and feelings about the Lord.

"I like how He fed all those people with the boy's lunch," Jason replied.

"That was one way Jesus showed people He loved them," Dad said. "Tell me some other things you like about Him."

"'Cause He loves everybody," Jason suggested.

"That's a good answer, Jason. I love Jesus very much, because I know He loves me."

"I love Jesus, too," said Jason.

"Let's tell Jesus that we love Him." After simple prayers were said by father and son, Dad asked, "Jason, do you want to talk about this some more right now, or do you want to do it tonight at bedtime?" Jason had had enough for one session and ran outside.

That night, Dad asked Jason, "Do you remember what we said about Jesus this afternoon? Do you want to talk about Him some more?" Jason did. So Dad said, "We talked about loving Jesus. Tell me what people do when they love someone."

Jason thought. "They do kind stuff. They help them."

"That's right, Jason. Now tell me what happens if someone does something to a person that makes that person unhappy."

"You have to say you're sorry," was Jason's reply.

"Tell me what it means to be sorry," Dad asked.

"Sorry means you are sad you did something, and won't do it again," Jason said.

Dad looked straight into Jason's eyes. "Now I'm going to ask you a hard question. Have you ever done anything that made Jesus unhappy?"

This question led Jason to confess several acts he believed were wrong. It was an easy step to lead Jason to a prayer in which he said he was sorry for what he had done wrong.

"Jason, Jesus loves you very much, even when you do something bad. But I am sure He is very happy because you have told Him you are sorry for those things. Let's talk about this again in a few days."

By this time, Jason had indicated that he knew the difference between right and wrong, and had an awareness of the effects of his actions. More important, he seemed eager to do the right thing instead of the wrong.

At the next conversation on this subject, Jason's dad asked, "Why do people need God to forgive them?" Jason was stymied here, so his dad explained to him how God wanted to help people do the right things instead of the wrong things. He raised the question again several days later. Jason explained in his five-year-old vocabulary his need for forgiveness. To be sure that Jason was not just repeating words he had heard, his dad phrased the question differently. "Tell me what happens to a boy who asks God to forgive him." When Jason seemed unsure, Dad explained, "When God forgives us, it means He will treat us just as though we had never done those wrong things. And it means we get to be part of God's own family." Dad showed Jason the place in the Bible where it says people can "become children of God" (John 1:12). This seemed to be enough new information at one time, so again the subject was held over until another day.

Each time the two talked about Jesus, Dad was careful to ask Jason if he wanted to talk about Him some more. If not, assurance was given that anytime Jason wanted to, Dad would be willing. Also, whenever Jason used a theological term, such as "saved," "forgiven" or "into my heart," Dad would ask Jason to tell him some more about that word. Whenever Dad thought he needed to clarify an idea for Jason, that idea would be considered again in the next conversation to see if Jason really understood.

The day Jason and his dad finally knelt down and Jason specifically asked to become part of God's family was certainly memorable. But it was not the first time they had prayed about such things. Nor was it the last, for Jason's father was equally concerned about nurturing Jason's growing understandings about being a Christian as he had been in helping Jason to make his own clearly understood commitment to Jesus Christ.

How Valid Is a Child's Decision?

After reading about Jason and his dad, some people ask, "But does that mean Jason is really born again?" Because of the limits of a child's understanding and experience, has the child truly become a Christian? Two questions need to be considered to evaluate the validity of a child's decision to become a Christian.

First, can a valid spiritual work be accomplished in a child's life even though the child may not understand much of what is involved? Fortunately, this is a matter that can and must be left to God. We need not fear that God will exclude anyone from His love because of less than perfect ability to understand. As Abraham once asked, "Will not the Judge of all the earth do right?" (Gen. 18:25).

Second, what should our response be to a child's decision? Leaving the theological arena for a moment, consider some other decisions a child might announce.

The little boy who declares that he is going to marry the girl next door does not elicit strenuous objections from family members trying to convince him he is far too young to think of such a thing. On the other hand, his father does not rush out to make reservations for the honeymoon. Similarly, the little girl who declares she is going to win an Olympic gold medal in figure skating is not met by protests that she can't even roller skate very well. Neither, however, does her mother immediately start looking for skating coaches in the Yellow Pages while her father starts making hotel reservations for the next five winter Olympics. In these typical situations, adults understand that the child is thinking ahead to the future, imagining what life might be like as he or she grows up.

Similarly, the child who announces a desire to become a Christian should not be treated as though his or her spiritual future is now firmly settled, but neither should the child's desire be belittled. At the very least, the child is showing an interest in spiritual matters, an attraction to the person of Jesus and a desire to do what God has instructed. Such a response by a child at any age deserves all the loving support, encouragement and continued guidance that parents and teachers can offer.

Notes

1. F. W. Eastman, "Children's Questions and Comments About the Christian Faith," *Religious Education* 58 (1963): 549.
2. Eleanor Zimmerman, *Doctrine for 3's to 5's* (Philadelphia: Lutheran Church Press, 1963), p. 103.
3. John Krahn, "Death and the Five- and Six-Year-Old," *Lutheran Education* (September 1973): 49-54.

The Child and God

"Who made God?"

"Nobody made God. He has always been alive."

"But, how did He get borned?"

"God isn't like us. He didn't have to be born. He has always been alive."

"But,...but,...but, who made Him?"

"This is very hard to understand, isn't it? There are many things about God I don't understand yet. All I know is that God was alive before anything else."

"But how did He get Hisself?"

Trying to answer the persistent questions of a child can often exhaust an adult's resources. Most children have more questions than adults have answers, especially when the subject is God. Probably no concept challenges the limits of human intelligence and imagination more than the idea of God. Every civilization of history has wrestled with the idea of God. The greatest minds of all time have struggled to understand the infinite.

How, then, can a young child, who is just being introduced to the reality of daily life, be expected to fathom such an immense concept? Why should anyone even mention God to a child whose limited experience virtually guarantees a significant amount of misunderstanding or confusion?

A child's eagerness to know about things usually stimulates thinking and a host of questions. Out of this curiosity, the child begins to want to know where things originate. The birth of a baby, the growth of a flower, the warm sun or chilling wind can all be the events that will stimulate extensive or momentary searches for answers.

Adults who possess a Christian faith of any degree, and who often feel puzzled about ways to answer children's questions, sometimes find it easy to simply reply, "God made it." This seems to satisfy most preschool-age inquirers for the moment, and the adult can return to other matters, at least until the next question surfaces.

Such answers are also given by parents and teachers who want children to begin learning about God as early as possible and to build a foundation for later Christian growth. Whatever the motive, much information the child receives about God will not be easily understood. Because the child cannot see or hear God, not many direct, physical experiences help to correct inaccurate concepts about what God is really like.

Many children arrive at an idea of what God is like early in life and then have little reason to alter that view in succeeding years. Without direct experience to modify or expand a level of understanding, the child is confined to a concept that does not mature. Many people who work with adolescents and young adults find that young people who turn away from Christianity are no longer satisfied by their childish misconceptions of God, but have nothing more complete to put in its place. To such young people, the idea of God is relegated to the dustbin of childish myths—along with Santa Claus, the Easter bunny and the tooth fairy.

This problem calls for parents and teachers to carefully analyze what children actually do think about God and how they develop their concepts, as well as ways of helping to prepare them for more mature understandings. A comment by an early-childhood specialist may serve as a word of caution before approaching this task: Could it be possible that the angels snicker at our "mature" ideas of God in the same way we find the ideas of young children so naively amusing?

The Child's Attitude About God

A child's attitude is far more significant and enduring than his or her level of understanding. Errors in knowledge can be corrected more easily than negative feelings can be changed. Obviously, the two areas are closely related and each has an influence upon the other. Especially in the early years of life, however, the child's reasoning abilities are severely limited and emotional qualities are more vital than at any other stage of development.

When a child thinks about God, his or her ideas may be immature, somewhat vague and often contradictory. But the child's feelings about God are usually quite definite. Some children learn at a very young age to fear God as a powerful judge who will punish them for any wrongdoing. The child who is consistently disciplined by threats, yelling and harsh punishments will begin to think of God as angry and vengeful. Others learn to associate God with all the good experiences of their lives and consider Him a helpful friend and concerned with their well-being.

Almost all children regard God with a great deal of awe, wonder and a certain degree of nervous uncertainty. In spite of what a particular child may say about God's actions, a basic emotional tone will underlie the surface beliefs, sometimes having a totally opposite meaning.[1]

The child's underlying attitude toward God is primarily formed in the process of interacting with adults, especially parents (see chapter 3). Although God is always seen as more powerful than Dad and Mom, the kind of relationship the child has with his or her parents dominates any impressions of God. As the child's thinking matures, many feelings about parents are gradually transferred to the child's feelings about God.[2] The inevitable misunderstandings about God can be minimized, or at least survived, if the child's attitudes have been shaped in a wholesome environment.

Parents who regularly lose their tempers with their children build an image of God as irritable. A string of broken promises, inconsistent standards and hypocritical morality leave the child with uncertain feelings about parents, and also with a concept of an unreliable God. Expressions of love, respect for the child's interest, consistent and reasonable discipline, and ethical behavior all combine to provide a positive base for a positive concept of God. Inevitable misunderstandings about God can be minimized, or at least survived, if the child has this solid, wholesome environment to shape his or her attitudes.

The Child's Thoughts About God

A distinguishing feature of children's ideas of God is the almost universal view of Him as having a somewhat human form. Although they recognize His great power, children consistently picture God as an old man in flowing robes with a long white beard "longer than Santa Claus's beard." A great deal of childish imagination is evident in any collection of children's descriptions of God, whether verbal or pictorial. He may be the strongest of men, or greater than any person could be. But He is still, in the child's final analysis, a physical being having all of the characteristics of humanity.[3]

God is good. Although the child will say that everything God does is good, certain actions of God are sometimes seen as somewhat suspect. Children seem to believe that God is similar to adults who often do strange things for no apparent reason, even though the child is told parents know what is best. Children may accept that dictum at face value. They will vigorously object in certain specific situations, however, when adult behavior does not fit the best plan of action as viewed by the child.

Part of the child's problem in distinguishing whether God, or a parent, has done the right thing is the difficulty the child has in acknowledging another person's point of view. The child frequently reads his or her own motivations into a description of God's actions. Very logically, the child will conclude that God acts in a manner similar to how he or she would act. References to God's anger are interpreted in terms of childish behavior such as becoming upset or frustrated. Thus, from a child's perspective, God changes His mind and makes mistakes, but at the same time the child affirms belief in God's perfection.[4]

God is everywhere. Many children seem to understand the concept of God's omnipresence, which is usually a comfort in times of stress. But the concept is so dominated by the child's reliance on physical qualities that the results are often somewhat ludicrous. "Is God really right here with us? Is He hiding behind the curtains? Is He in my pockets?" The nonphysical nature of God baffles the child.

God as spirit. Even when a child can use "correct" terms to describe God as a spirit, the understanding of those words is very limited. Six-year-old Stephanie could say, "God is a spirit." When asked what that meant, she could explain, "That means He doesn't have a body." But when pushed another step to tell something else about God, she described Him as, "He wears a long white robe, and has a beard and a mustache." Neither the words she had learned nor the explanations she had been taught were enough to take Stephanie beyond the natural limits of having to think concretely and physically. She had to visualize this Being without a body as wearing clothing and having a luxurious beard.

God's power. The literal quality of a child's thinking creates problems in understanding God's use of His power. Children often see Him utilizing His "hands" and "arms" or applying levitation in a manner similar to a magician. They expect God to work on external situations. For example, it is not uncommon for a young child to interpret the idea of God's care to mean that God would provide safe passage in crossing the street by stopping the cars.

God's love. Children also seem thoroughly convinced that God loves everyone. In a specific situation, however, they may easily affirm that one individual or group is favored more than another. In many Bible stories, it appears to a child that the "heroes" deserve love more than the "villains." In everyday life, for example, a child really is convinced of being loved more by God than others are. Usually, a child's close family and friends are also included in this elite circle of God's most special people.

Again, a limited view of life hems a child into only one perspective. A child may earnestly declare that God equally loves boys and girls in other countries, but such words are only an inaccurate gauge of the child's true feelings.

Heaven. Heaven also comes in for its share of childish imaginings. To the child, it is a physical place, located somewhere in the sky, often in or above the clouds. For some children, heaven is a vague and misty abode for that strange man, God. Others conjure delightful visions of a spectacular playground where children are free to do everything they want. Heaven's desirabilities are not usually sufficient to make the child really want to go there. But it does serve as a useful catchall to locate any departed pets or relatives.[5]

In most Christian homes, God is not an integral part of the child's day-by-day experiences. Except for meal and bedtime prayers and an occasional Bible story, He is comfortably removed from the life of the child. To a large extent, this pattern results from parents not relating God to the important moments of their own lives. The child and the adult both tend to be too dominated by immediate physical perceptions to be overly concerned with a God who has never actually been seen.

Activities for Learning About God

The Effect of Love and Discipline
Adults who desire to provide positive models to enhance children's atti-

tudes and understandings of God should give special attention to two areas of their relationships with a child: love and discipline. Ultimately, everything dealt with in this book comes down to a question of how these two vital needs of the child are met.

Love. The vast majority of adults who work closely with children claim to love them. However, child abuse and neglect are rarely, if ever, inflicted by people who say they hate kids. The worst trauma of abuse is not the physical injury, but the betrayal by a person the child looked to for care and protection.

The adult's profession of love is not the issue. The point is this: Does the child really feel loved? Love for the child is very physical. Cuddling and patting are important for both boys and girls, which makes sexual abuse of children all the more heinous because it betrays a deep-seated need of the child. Love consists of adults noticing the child and participating in things the child enjoys. Love also needs to be verbal. Words need to accompany the hugs, pats and smiles, reinforcing the value and worth the adult sees in the child.

Expressions of love must not be held hostage by the adult's moods or the child's behavior. To receive love, a child should not have to depend on earning it, for love is much too fragile for such a condition to exist. For if love can be earned, it can also be lost. A child's fear of losing someone's love creates tension, not assurance.

Discipline. Discipline, which encompasses far more than punishment, is the process of molding attitudes and behavior in a careful and loving manner. Harsh or inconsistent methods, even with the best of intentions, result in frustration and resentment—the very things the apostle Paul warned parents not to arouse: *"Fathers, do not exasperate your children; instead, bring them up in the training and instruction of the Lord"* (Eph. 6:4, italics added). Proper discipline is firm but patient.

Unfortunately, God is often introduced into the discipline of young children as a threat—a sad mistake indeed! The parent who resorts to threatening a child with God's displeasure is revealing his or her own weakness to the child.[6] This kind of discipline diminishes the respect the child has for the adult and for God. Negative feelings toward a God who is used as a threat will linger long after the specific incident has been forgotten.

In contrast, when adults offer guidelines that are reasonable and logical, the child develops the ability to make wise choices. Also, the child's view of the adult as a guide and helper is strengthened.

The word "discipline" does not mean punishment. It means "teaching" or "instruction"—and there is a big difference between the two. The adult who reacts to misbehavior by venting anger and frustration may succeed in getting the child to stop, at least temporarily, the unwanted actions. But the adult who responds by patiently and firmly guiding the child to correct the misbehavior and replace it with positive actions is helping the child learn the right way to live.

Relating God to a Child's Experience

To help the child recognize God's presence and interest in everyday experiences, introduce God into conversations while the child is in the midst of a specific activity. The child who is sitting passively in a chair in Sunday School will simply not comprehend the teacher's assurances of God's presence during the week. Both the child's difficulty in transferring learning from one situation to another, as well as the distance in both space and time from the actual situation, will leave the child with only vague and often fanciful ideas about what the teacher meant. It is far better to focus first on an awareness of God's presence in the middle of the child's current activity, and then mention that God is also present in all other times and places. For example, little Aaron was perfectly logical in blaming God for his misbehavior one day. "I asked God to help me be good, so it's His fault that I talked back to Mommy!"

Fortunately, Aaron's mother recognized that her son was not guilty of blasphemy, but was simply coming to a logical conclusion from the limited information he had been given. She tried to help him correct his thinking by saying, "Aaron, God won't make us do anything. But I have found that when I really want to do the right thing, asking God to help me do it makes it easier. If I want to do something bad, God won't make me do something else."

This conversation with Aaron, in the middle of a very real encounter, helped him clarify the concept. Although there can be no firm assurance that he fully grasped his mother's meaning, he is closer to it than he would have been if the same information was handed to him apart from the specific situation. More important, Aaron's mother is establishing a pattern of answering his questions and responding to his statements. Giving attention to a child's interests strengthens parent/child relationships.

Karen's father frequently took her to a nearby park where they enjoyed many activities. Frequent opportunities to mention God in natural and specific ways occurred during these excursions. One day while looking at the park's rose garden in full bloom, her father asked, "What would you think if there were no such things as flowers?"

"Then the park wouldn't be pretty," Karen answered.

"And what if there weren't any flowers anywhere?"

"I wouldn't like that. I think flowers are nice."

"So do I," said Dad. "Aren't we glad God made flowers for us to enjoy?"

On another occasion, Karen asked, "Did God make the swings and the slide?"

"What do you think?" Dad asked.

Karen thought a moment, then answered, "I think some people made them."

"You're right. When God first made the world, He made people so we can think and plan and work. God knew that we would need to build houses and other buildings. And I think He knew that little girls would like to play on swings and slides."

Answering Questions

The child's questions are one of the best indicators of the child's level of thinking. The kinds of questions the child asks assist adults in knowing how much information about God is appropriate at the time. The problem most adults face is in determining if their answers are adequate. Again, the child's queries and comments are usually a good barometer.

Many teachers do as Karen's father did, and respond to a question with a question. Guiding the child to think about his or her own inquiry can help both parent and child think more clearly about the problem at hand. Another helpful approach is to follow an answer with a question to see how the child reacted to the new information.

After Mrs. Anderson would answer a question from her kindergartners, she would often ask, "What do you think of that answer?" She wisely sought to use her answers to stimulate further thought.

Be cautious about assuming that a child's question is an opportunity to expound on everything known about that topic. One dad, while driving home from church with his daughter, who was in the back seat of the car, thought her question deserved a detailed explanation. So as he drove across town, he explained, and explained and explained. Stopping at a red light, he glanced in the mirror to see how his daughter was receiving all this enlightened information, and was surprised that she was not in sight. He looked over his shoulder, then down behind the front seat. To his consternation, she was sitting on the floor and had her hands clasped firmly over her ears!

A good rule of thumb is to give a one-sentence answer to a one-sentence question. Then check with the child to see if he or she wants to hear any more information.

Questions and Answers About God

What do you say to a child's questions about God? For the answers to be meaningful, they must fit the child's present level of understanding. They must also fit the adult who is answering. For example, an adult who is cold and distant will probably have little success in explaining how God loves the child. A loving and understanding adult might speak the same words, but the effect that answer would have on the child would be entirely different. The attitude of the adult makes the difference.

Admit when you do not know the answer. Any answer to a child's question about God should make sense to the adult and not just be an attempt to parrot what is presumed to be the "right" answer. Giving an answer the adult does not really believe can only make the discussion about God hypocritical. The child is bound to discover the discrepancy sooner or later. It is more preferable to say, "I don't know. There are many things about God that nobody really knows." One father responded to a knotty question this way, "I just don't know how to answer that. It's a good question, but I'm going to have to think about it for a few days. I might even ask someone else. I promise I'll do my best to find the answer for you."

Avoid overly simplistic or fanciful answers—the kind the child will have to unlearn in later years. Give the briefest, most accurate answer to a question possible, then ask, "Was that a good answer?" The child will let you know if he or she wants to know more.

A few typical questions children ask:

What does God look like? One teacher answered this way, "No one has ever seen God, so we don't know what He looks like. The Bible does talk about Him sometimes as though He looks like a man. That helps us to be able to think about Him."

Where does God live? A possible answer is, "God is everywhere, all at the same time. No one understands how He does that, but we know it is true." This answer may not fully satisfy the child, but it is preferable to locating God in a faraway "heaven." Also, leaving the child with the reality of mystery provides a means for avoiding simplistic answers that become locked in as the child grows older.

Where is heaven? is similar to the previous question. The child hears the term used in sentences as a place name and assumes it is a physical location. Because the young child cannot comprehend the nonphysical, this question drives parents to seek help from "experts," or to seek refuge in a simple answer, "It's up in the sky." This answer runs into problems, however, when the child takes an airplane ride or watches rocket launchings on television. One parent preferred to answer this way: "Heaven is real, but no one on earth has ever seen it. The Bible tells us that heaven is wonderful. But heaven is so different from anything we know that it's hard for us to understand what it's like." This does not free the child from physical conceptualization, but at least it removes heaven from the path of a jetliner.

When will I go to heaven? One teacher simply said, "I don't know. It's not time yet for that to happen."

How does God take care of me? is the subject of an infinite variety of questions about God's role in the child's life. The best answers focus the child's attention on God's specific provisions for human sustenance. "God made the whole world with all the plants and animals we would need to live. And God planned for people to have strong bodies to use these things that He made for us. And he planned for us to have families and friends so we can help each other." This answer helps the child to appreciate the abilities God has given, and to be grateful for people who are part of his or her life. It also helps the child to avoid the fanciful view that God protects by magical means, removing responsibility from the individual.

Does God get mad? is the kind of question that explores God's response to the child's action. The child's interpretation of anger is totally conditioned by the expressions of it being experienced in interactions with other people. One of the nicest answers was given by Andrea's grandmother. "God loves you so much, Andrea, that He always wants you to do what is best so you and everyone else will be happy. When you do something that isn't the best, God is sad, for He knows you won't really be happy because of that."

Notes

1. Ronald Goldman, *Religious Thinking from Childhood to Adolescence* (New York: Seabury Press, 1964), p. 140.

2. Jean Piaget, *The Child's Conception of the World* (Lanham, Md.: Littlefield, 1975), p. 354.

3. Ibid., p. 382.

4. Goldman, *Religious Thinking from Childhood to Adolescence*, p. 126.

5. Ibid., p. 89.

6. C. A. Nunve, "Child Control Through a 'Coalition with God,'" *Child Development* 35 (1964): 417.

Learning that Makes a Difference

"What did you learn in Sunday School this morning, Eugene?"

(Silence)

"What was the Bible story your teacher told?"

"I don't remember."

"Do you remember anything that happened?"

(Silence)

"You know, Eugene, your teacher told me you were just full of wiggles this morning. Did you have a hard time sitting still?"

"Yes."

"Eugene, no wonder you didn't learn anything. You know we take you to Sunday School to learn about God."

"But my teacher made me stay in my chair, and she teached, and teached, and I got so tired I just couldn't learn anything!"

Learning is a full-time job for children. For young children, everything in their world is so new and interesting that they continually feel a compulsion to explore and experiment. Older children possess an energy and a rapidly growing store of knowledge and experience that motivates continued interest in making new discoveries. Even before language becomes operative, every child possesses opinions, feelings, beliefs and information on a wide range of subjects. The child's continuous learning contributes to a developing personality structure that identifies him or her as a unique person.

Principles for Guiding Spiritual Development

Considering that knowledge at birth is zero, the quantity and quality of learning a child accumulates in a few short years is truly remarkable. It is especially noteworthy to recognize that the prime director of this learning process is the child! The child learns what the child experiences. The child's interests, abilities and attention span are the dominant factors in making sense out of the maze of daily experiences. Although parents, peers and teachers provide many of the ingredients for these experiences, the child sets the pace for his or her own learning program.[1]

Enjoyment

The child applies the same control and technique in the area of spiritual development as in any other dimension of learning. The child takes from every conversation, song, story and lesson those aspects he or she finds interesting and meaningful, regardless of adult intentions.

A Sunday School teacher was seeking to impress her five-year-olds with the significance of the Ten Commandments. As the children grew increasingly restless, she patiently explained each of the concepts involved. Realizing that her young charges did not seem to be appreciating the great truths she was sharing, she asked, "If you were asked to make up ten commandments that would help everyone be happy and live together the right way, what would you think would be most important?"

Gregory came to life. "Thou shalt have fun," he declared firmly.

Theologians might dispute Gregory's commandment. However, although he may not know theology, he certainly knows children. The vast majority of the miscellaneous, but essential, learning the child accomplishes depends to a large extent on the degree of enjoyment of the learning task.[2] No child would learn to talk if the ability to communicate were not perceived as desirable. Why do all normal babies exert themselves to roll over, sit up, crawl and finally walk? Babies do these things because of the great satisfaction in seeing the world from a new perspective. Each child gains a splendid feeling of achievement in being able to do something new. And, or course, Mom and Dad get so excited about each new trick that the child becomes motivated to do things just to see adult reactions.

Unfortunately, much of the pure pleasure of learning goes out the window when people approach the child's Christian education. Suddenly, parents and teachers begin talking about things the child "ought to know," and have little consideration for whether the child "wants to know." Comments such as "It's for her own good" and "They'll appreciate it when they're older" reflect typical adult thinking. Thus, the child's religious instruction takes on all the qualities of administering a dose of castor oil, often with the same kind of reaction by the child. Or, just as damaging, many adults who sense that children do not respond well to "force-feeding the faith," simply give up altogether or assign their child's religious nurture to professionals.

How can adults talk about faith as the essential ingredient of a happy satisfying life, then either make teaching it to children an endurance contest or ignore it altogether? How can anyone justify either boring children with the Bible or letting the Book gather dust throughout the childhood years? Christian faith, if it is to enrich the lives of children now and through their future years, must be taught with delight and joy. The method must fit the objective.

Relationships

The most effective method for teaching Christian concepts to a child is for adults whose faith makes a difference in the quality of their lives to build a positive relationship with the child. Each concept considered in this book is more effectively communicated to a child through the relationships the child experiences than through any verbal explanations.[3]

The attitude of the child is of far greater consequence than knowledge of specific facts or ideas. Developing positive, healthy feelings and values should be of much greater concern to parents and teachers than the child's ability to recite verses or recount information. Surrounding the child with secure and loving relationships with understanding Christians is an essential foundation for effectively sharing a faith that centers on a personal relationship with Jesus Christ. Building a relationship with a child is not a method to make the child receptive to the important stuff we want to communicate. Relationships are the essence of what Christianity is all about.

Thought Depends on Action

Those who guide a child's spiritual development need to keep in mind that the child's thought processes are dependent upon accompanying action.[4] The child's ability to reason and understand grows through real-life experiences that call into play the physical senses. Simply talking about Christian ways of living, for example, does not provide the child with ample input to develop valid, realistic concepts. The child needs repeated and varied opportunities to put specific Bible truths into action in real or simulated experiences. The child needs to feel what it's like to have received as well as to give, if a verse such as "Freely you have received, freely give" (Matt. 10:8) is to have any meaning.

Parents have many opportunities during the course of family activities to make their own values evident to the child. Everyday experiences provide material for meaningful conversations, however brief, pointing out the parents' motives and attitudes. Teachers who work with children in the more artificial setting of a classroom need to plan and create situations in which the child can learn through firsthand experiences.

Response to Children's Questions

Allow a child's questions to guide the direction and level of learning situations. Typically, adults tend to organize information *logically*, presenting an orderly outline of subject matter. The child's learning needs to be structured *psychologically*, however, moving with the everchanging interests of the child.[5]

Jesus frequently used this method by tailoring His discussions to the questions asked by His listeners. Even the New Testament Epistles were not written as step-by-step essays on religion. They were written in response to real questions and real problems that were being raised among the real people of the young churches of the Apostolic Age.

A child proceeds with learning in much the same way—asking questions to help solve current problems. The child does not wait to learn a new word until easier ones have all been mastered. Nor does he or she wait to try running until walking is successfully under control. The child works on whatever is at hand, whatever appears of interest. As a result, the child learns many things in what appears to be a highly unorganized approach. Some educators criticize teachers of young children for "trying to teach all things to all children all the time." The approach of these teachers, however, deals with children the way they learn best. It may not be systematic, but it works!

Adults need to give the child exposure to many situations, stimulating interest and questions, then answer those questions in ways to further spark the child's thinking. Avoid the desire to follow up the child's question with complete coverage of the subject at hand. Rather, develop the skill of sensing the amount of information the child wants at the moment, and satisfy only that much. Trying to give a child more information than is desired has a deadening effect on the child's interest in further learning.

Repetition

Repetition is also an essential ingredient in a child's learning process. When an activity is fun for a child, the watchword is "Do it again." Children need opportunities to repeat their learning in a variety of ways. For example, when a kindergarten teacher is presenting a unit of lessons involving sharing, he or she will provide learning activities—firsthand experiences—that encourage sharing. The pictures will illustrate sharing situations and the conversation will focus on that concept as the teacher reinforces desirable behaviors. *Be generous and willing to share* (1 Tim. 6:18) might be the Bible verse the teacher uses as the children's thoughts and words are guided.

Adults often tire of the simplicity of many childish games and interests. Adults want a change from stories they feel are overly familiar. Instead of focusing on the content or the activity, however, adults should concentrate on the wonder in the child's eyes, the joy of insight and discovery. Sharing in a child's learning then becomes one of life's most rewarding opportunities for adult renewal. The parent or teacher who enters enthusiastically into repeated, familiar experiences with a child often learns more from observing the child than the child learns from the adult.

Molding a young child's knowledge and attitude about God is truly an awesome responsibility. Jesus believed this strongly enough to declare, "But if anyone causes one of these little ones who believe in me to sin, it would be better for him to have a large millstone hung around his neck and to be drowned in the depths of the sea" (Matt. 18:6).

Why such a stern warning? Is it because in guiding a child we have the future in our grasp? Is it because the young child is so trusting that he or she will confidently follow our guidance? Is it because children are in some way so important to God that He thus gives them this special concern?

A few verses later, Jesus followed that admonition with a powerful message of encouragement, "Your Father in heaven is not willing that any of these little ones should be lost" (v. 14). Imagine! The person who is committed to nurturing the spiritual life of a child is working in cooperation with the will of God the Father!

Because God earnestly desires that children grow to love and worship Him, He offers all the help needed to anyone who shares His longing for guiding children. Whether you are a parent or a teacher, you can enjoy the extraordinary adventure of working in partnership with God!

God has made even the youngest child curious and ready to learn. What the child learns and how you help this process is up to you. And you can't begin too soon!

Notes

1. H. Munsinger, *Fundamentals of Child Development* (New York: Holt, Rinehart and Winston, 1971), p. 124.
2. Ibid., p. 106.
3. Eleanor Zimmerman, *Doctrine for 3's to 5's* (Philadelphia: Lutheran Church Press, 1963), p. 7.
4. David Elkind, "The Origins of Religion in the Child," *Review of Religious Research* 12 (1970): 36.
5. R. S. Lee, *Your Growing Child and Religion* (New York: MacMillan, 1964), p. 160.

For Further Reading

Armsby, R. E. "A Re-examination of the Development of Moral Judgment in Children." *Child Development* 42 (1971).

Briggs, Dorothy C. *Your Child's Self-Esteem: The Key to His Life.* New York: Doubleday, 1970.

Childers, P., and M. Wimmer. "The Concept of Death in Early Childhood." *Child Development* 42 (1971).

Coles, R. "The Moral Life of Children." *Atlantic Monthly* (1985).

Cowles, M. "Four Views of Learning and Development." *Education Leadership* 28 (1971).

Cox, E. "Honest to Goldman: An Assessment." *Religious Education* 63 (1968).

Dobson, J. *Hide or Seek.* Grand Rapids: Fleming H. Revell, 1974.

Eastman, F. W. "Children's Questions and Comments About the Christian Faith." *Religious Education* 58 (1963).

Elkind, David. "The Origins of Religion in the Child." *Review of Religious Research* 12 (1970).

— — —. *Understanding Your Child from Birth to Sixteen.* Boston: Allyn and Bacon, 1994.

Erikson, Erik. *Childhood and Society.* 2nd ed. New York: W. W. Norton, 1963.

Gardner, Howard. *The Unschooled Mind.* New York: Basic Books, 1991.

Ginsburg, H., and S. Opper. *Piaget's Theory of Intellectual Development: An Introduction.* 3rd ed. Englewood Cliffs, N.J.: Prentice Hall, 1990.

Goldman, Ronald. *Readiness for Religion.* New York: Seabury Press, 1965.

Graebner, O. E. "Child Concepts of God." *Religious Education* 59 (1964).

Haystead, Wesley. *Everything You Want to Know About Teaching Young Children: Birth—6 Years.* Ventura, Calif.: Regal Books, 1989.

Hendricks, W. *A Theology for Children.* Nashville: Broadman Press, 1980.

Kohlberg, Lawrence. "Development of Moral Character and Moral Ideology" in *Review of Child Development Research.* eds. M. Hoffman and L. Hoffman, vol. 1. New York: Russell Sage Foundation, 1964.

Krahn, John. "A Comparison of Kohlberg's and Piaget's Type I Morality." *Religious Education* 66 (1971).

Lawrence, P. J. "Children's Thinking About Religion: A Study of Concrete Operational Thinking." *Religious Education* 60 (1965).

Maslow, A. H. *Motivation and Personality.* New York: HarperCollins, 1954.

Miller, K. *The Becomers.* Dallas: Word Inc., 1973.

Munsinger, H. *Fundamentals of Child Development.* New York: Holt, Rinehart and Winston, 1971.

Nordberg, R. B. "Developing the Idea of God in Children." *Religious Education* 66 (1971).

O'Neill, R. P., and M. A. Donovan. *Children, Church and God: The Case Against Formal Religious Education.* New York: Corpus Books, 1970.

Piaget, Jean. *The Moral Judgment of the Child.* Glencoe, Ill.: Free Press, 1948.

— — —. *Origins of Intelligence.* New York: International Universities Press, 1964.

— — —. *Science of Education and the Psychology of the Child.* New York: Orion Press, 1970.

Sholl, D. "The Contributions of Lawrence Kohlberg to Religious and Moral Education." *Religious Education* 66 (1971).

Siegler, R. S. *Children's Thinking.* Englewood Cliffs, N.J.: Prentice Hall, 1991.

Tizard, B., and M. Hughes. *Young Children Learning.* Cambridge, Mass.: Harvard University Press, 1984.

Zimmerman, Eleanor. *Doctrine for 3's to 5's.* Philadelphia: Lutheran Church Press, 1963.